YOUR KITCHEN'S MAGIC WAND

Getting the Most
Out of Your
Handheld Immersion Blender

St. Martin's Press New York

YOUR KITCHEN'S MAGIC WAND

TOM STEELE

Photographs by Rebecca Bent

Book design by Susan Walsh

Library of Congress Cataloging-in-Publication Data

Steele, Tom, 1952–
    Your kitchen's magic wand : getting the most out of your handheld immersion blender / by Tom Steele ; photographs by Rebecca Bent.
        p. cm.
    ISBN-13: 978-0-312-35541-8
    ISBN-10: 0-312-35541-6
    1. Blenders (Cookery) I. Title.

TX840.B5S74 2006
641.5'893—dc22

                                                            2006046419

First Edition: October 2006

10 9 8 7 6 5 4 3 2 1

To all the mothers and fathers who take the time and trouble to teach their children how to enjoy food and how to cook it, but in particular to my own mother, Suzanne Easton Steele-Mueller, who did precisely that, with love and considerable gusto.

CONTENTS

ACKNOWLEDGMENTS

I want to thank the many people who encouraged me to take this culinary direction in my life, in particular:

Elizabeth Beier, who came up with the idea for this book and really wanted me to write it, and who has become a cherished friend.

Rebecca Bent, who gave me my first real cookbook opportunity, who made the gorgeous photographs for this book, who is the crowned princess of multitasking, and who has also become a treasured friend.

My sensational family, in particular my sisters Rusty Levenson and Marcia Steele, my sister-in-law Lynn Haney, my nephews Moss and Cormac Levenson, my nieces Rachel Webster and Geddes Levenson, cousins Margo, Jim, and Megan Morrow, and, oh, everyone else.

Chuck Ortleb gave me my first food writing job, and millions of other opportunities before and after that.

My beloved friends Neenyah Ostrom, Tom Miller, Jim Pellegrinon, Tadhg O'Connor, and Rodger Parsons all endured or enjoyed many of these recipes in turn and gave me acres of vital support.

Brendan Lemon has been steadfast in his enthusiasm for my work, and has provided me with important opportunities every step of the way.

The consistently amazing man I lived with for fifteen years, Raymond Luczak, shaped the way I cook in countless ways.

Adam Kowit provides vital feedback and encouragement on a charmingly regular basis.

INTRODUCTION

So you got yourself a nice new immersion blender? Say good-bye to lumpy gravies and polentas and sauces. With powerful surges, this highly maneuverable handheld thick wand with a blender blade whizzing at its submergible tip can ream the lumps out of an errant sauce in seconds—right in the hot saucepan. Need whipped cream for that pumpkin pie? You'll have it in a jiffy. Want to thicken soups without using cream or flour or cornstarch? Strain out a few cups of broth, puree a cup of cooked rice in the broth with a handheld blender, and return it to the soup. Presto! Got a child who's a fussy eater? Quickly puree those cooked vegetables she wouldn't touch with your immersion blender, stir the mixture into whatever soup she likes, and serve it for lunch. Want to make a smoothie right in the tumbler you'll drink it in? Cleanup is always a snap—literally—when it comes to using a handheld blender. The "business end" snaps off the motor/handle and rinses clean in seconds.

An immersion blender is at its best a multispeed electric motor with a rotating blade at its tip. The blade spins furiously in a plastic or metal hood. The speed of the rotation is controlled by a dial at the top of the blender, but the motor goes on only when a switch is pressed (on most models). When this spring-loaded switch is released, the motor stops. The handheld blender works equally well for right- and left-handed people.

Many of the recipes in this book would be a massive undertaking if you had to use a standing blender. In many of the preparatory phases, you'd have to stop and start at crucial points, rupturing the rhythm of your cooking, even risking overcooking. You usually have to scrape down the sides of an average blender to get an even puree. And because so many of the recipes involve working with a hot mixture, there's a constant risk of overfilling a conventional blender and having the resulting steam blow the lid off the blender, splattering you and everything in your kitchen. Not to mention that anyone who's ever cleaned a blender knows that you must disassemble the many parts and scrub with hot soapy water to keep the blender safe and clean. Cleaning a handheld immersion blender takes under five seconds. I like to keep a bowl of clean water at the ready, so that as soon as I've pureed my soup or sauce or dressing or coulis, I run the blender in the clean water, then unplug it and rinse the blade in hot water. I store my immersion blender in its two parts, wrapped in a clean dish towel.

Braun was the first company to manufacture an immersion blender, in the early 1980s, and leading chefs immediately hailed it as the greatest kitchen invention since the food processor came on the scene ten years earlier. Today there are dozens of models available, from KitchenAid to Cuisinart. Some would maintain that the original inventor continues to make the best appliance, and, in this case, I would agree, having tried all the leading immersion blenders in the course of writing this book. But all the electric models are good. Just be sure that your immersion blender has at least 200 watts of power and three or more speeds. Don't go for any battery-operated blender. You might as well use a miniature baseball bat.

You really don't need a bells-and-whistles model that comes with fairly useless attachments like whisks and awkward chopper heads, which seem particularly futile if you already have a miniprocessor. It *is* useful to have at least one cylindrical container that's an inch or so wider in diameter than the business end of your immersion blender. Such a vessel is particularly useful to puree small amounts of food in less than 1 cup of liquid, and also in making smoothies. Most immersion blenders of any stature come equipped with such a container.

Immersion blender splatters do happen, especially when you're blending in a wide, low pan or bowl. Perhaps, in their infinite wisdom, Braun et al. will come up with a splatter solution one day. Until then, you can use parchment paper: Cut a hole about ½ inch wider in diameter than the end of your immersion blender in a large square of parchment. Center the parchment over the bowl you're blending in, fasten it around the bowl with rubber bands, and blend away. Or saw a hole in the center of a new Frisbee. Remember, as long as you keep the vents that surround the rotating blade at the end of the stick blender *immersed* while using a gentle up-and-down motion, you won't have splatters. If you're an immersion blender virgin, I recommend practicing with a bowl of cold water. Submerge the head of the blender before turning on the motor, and avoid touching the blender to the bottom of the bowl and keep it slightly angled—sometimes the blender "sticks" due to the tremendous suction created by the madly whirring blade. If your blender has more than one speed—as well it should!—try starting out on a lower speed. If you're dealing with a small amount of liquid, simply tilt the vessel itself with your free hand to create a fully immersible level of liquid. If you're trying to incorporate air into a mixture, as for a smoothie or latte or whipped cream, hold the blender up to keep the blade whirring just under the surface of the liquid.

Immersion blenders are quite top-heavy, so never leave yours standing upright in a container. It will tip over sure as you're born. Instead, remove it from the container and lay it down on a work surface. Also, if you're pureeing hot soup or a sauce right in the pot, take it off the heat. A blender cord resting on a hot burner or burner guard could be dangerous.

There are some things an immersion blender can't do very well. It doesn't evenly chop ice or nuts or other hard dry foods, and even if yours can, you'll dull the rotary blade if you use it as a grinder. Plus, without liquid, the immersion blender can send bits of solid food flying around your kitchen. You *can* mash potatoes, but they come out a bit gluey. Better to use a ricer for the job. Also, the blender can toughen flour-heavy batters.

The world doesn't need another smoothie cookbook, and there are plenty of great soup cookbooks out there as well. While I've included several unusual recipes for both smoothies and soups, this book is mostly made up of the *best* starters and entrées that are made ever so much easier with an immersion blender. I wanted, above all, to show off the sheer versatility of the handheld blender.

STARTERS

Cucumber Rounds with Smoky Hummus and Soft Goat Cheese

These are absolutely addictive. Don't put them all out at once, or your guests won't have any room for dinner.

One 15-ounce can chickpeas, rinsed and drained
2 canned chipotle peppers, stemmed and seeded,
   with a teaspoon of the adobo they were canned with (if you
   like it hotter, add one more pepper)
1 large clove garlic, coarsely chopped
3 tablespoons fresh lemon juice
3 tablespoons tahini (mixed well before measuring)
2 tablespoons extra virgin olive oil
1 teaspoon ground cumin
Kosher salt
2 tablespoons water
1 large seedless cucumber (usually available plastic-wrapped at
   the supermarket)
½ cup soft plain goat cheese, such as chèvre, at room
   temperature
Thick plain yogurt, for garnish
3 tablespoons lightly toasted sesame seeds

Place the chickpeas, chipotles, garlic, lemon juice, tahini, olive oil, cumin, ¼ teaspoon salt, and 2 tablespoons water in a medium bowl just large enough to hold everything. Puree the ingredients with an immersion blender, scraping down the sides of the bowl as necessary, about 2 minutes, until the mixture is smooth and fluffy.

Use a vegetable peeler to peel the cucumber skin lengthwise at ¼-inch intervals to create a stripped pattern around the circumference of the cucumber, and slice it crosswise into ¼-inch rounds. Place the cucumber disks on a platter.

To assemble, lightly salt the cucumber rounds. Top each round with a smear of goat cheese, then a generous teaspoon of hummus, and top the hummus with a small dollop of the yogurt. Sprinkle the cucumber rounds lightly with the sesame seeds.

Yield: about 40 hors d'oeuvres

Chickpea, Roasted Pepper, and Rosemary Spread

This is a Middle Eastern dip with a savory American accent.

Two (15-ounce) cans chickpeas, drained
One 6-ounce jar roasted red peppers or pimientos, drained well,
    seeded, and coarsely chopped
Juice of ½ lemon
2 medium cloves garlic, pressed
2 tablespoons fresh rosemary leaves
Sea salt and freshly ground black pepper
2 tablespoons extra virgin olive oil
Lightly toasted pita bread triangles
1 large yellow and 1 large red bell pepper, stemmed, seeded,
    and sliced into lengthwise strips
1 pint cherry tomatoes, rinsed, stemmed, and halved

Combine the chickpeas, red peppers, lemon juice, garlic, rosemary, and salt and pepper in a medium bowl. Pulse the ingredients with an immersion blender for a few minutes, then add the olive oil and pulse until the mixture is smooth. Serve the mixture in a bowl on a platter, surrounding the bowl with the pita bread, yellow and red bell pepper strips, and cherry tomatoes.

Yield: 8 appetizer servings

Flaming Hot Peanuts

You can control the heat in these zippy peanuts by selecting a milder bottled sauce, but this recipe is really for people who like very spicy food. Write down your own approximate combinations for future reference, because people are going to want this recipe! Note: The peanuts need to be started two days before serving.

2 pounds dry-roasted, salted peanuts, such as Planter's
2 tablespoons Tabasco sauce
2 tablespoons peanut oil
Juice of 1 lime
2 teaspoons prepared sweet red pepper relish
¼ cup bottled or canned sliced jalapeños, drained
8 drops Liquid Smoke
Other hot sauce(s) of your choice
2 dozen dried chiles de arbol, stemmed and broken into ½ inch
    pieces (optional)

Pour the peanuts into a large sealable plastic bag. In a 1-cup glass measure, place the Tabasco, oil, lime juice, red pepper relish, jalapeños, and Liquid Smoke. Add the other hot sauce(s) of your choice to fill the measuring cup to the brim. Transfer the mixture to a small bowl and roughly puree with an immersion blender.

Pour the sauce over the peanuts in the bag, press the air out of the bag, seal it, and squish it around to mix well. Marinate overnight, refrigerated, turning the bag a few times.

Heat the oven to 250°F. Line a baking sheet or jelly-roll pan with parchment paper or a Silpat mat. Spread the peanuts over the sheet. Roast gently for 2½ to 3 hours, stirring every half hour. Turn the oven off, and let the peanuts rest in the oven overnight to dry out.

Toss the peanuts with the optional chiles de arbol, and keep in airtight container(s) lined with paper towels.

Yield: 2 pounds hot peanuts

Tomato Flans

This summery flan is delicious as a first course with toasted Tuscan bread or as a restorative lunch with a lightly dressed tumble of mesclun. If the flan doesn't unmold symmetrically, you can easily reshape it with a spoon for presentation's sake. I find that using a Silpat mold doesn't work at all. It won't release the flans.

2 cloves garlic
2 medium dead-ripe tomatoes, peeled, seeded, and chopped, or one 8-ounce can tomato sauce, preferably Muir Glen organic
10 large basil leaves
¼ cup peeled, seeded, and diced cucumber
¼ cup extra virgin olive oil
2 teaspoons balsamic vinegar
1 teaspoon dark brown sugar
1 tablespoon plus 1 teaspoon unflavored gelatin powder (about 1⅓ envelopes)
Salt and freshly ground white pepper to taste
Canola oil, for oiling the ramekins
Mint sprigs, for garnish (optional)

Press the garlic cloves through a sturdy garlic press into a 4-cup glass measure and immediately pour in the tomatoes or tomato sauce. Add the basil leaves, cucumber, olive oil, balsamic vinegar, brown sugar, gelatin, and salt and white pepper to taste. With an immersion blender, puree the mixture at high speed for 2 minutes, or until very smooth.

Lightly oil six ½-cup glass or glazed ramekins. Divide the

tomato mixture among the ramekins and refrigerate them for at least 20 minutes. Cover each ramekin with plastic wrap if you're refrigerating them for much longer.

To serve, dip the bottom of each cup in hot water to loosen the flan. Place a plate over each mold and invert the ramekins over the plates to unmold the flans. Garnish with mint sprigs, if desired, and droplets of olive oil.

Yield: 6 servings

Baba Ghanoush with Toasted Pine Nuts

This fabled dip demonstrates how well an immersion blender lets you control the texture of a dish. I find that white eggplant brings a certain subtle sweetness to the dip, but you can also use classic purple eggplant. If you want to take the Baba to spicy Mexico, add the chipotles. If not, leave them out. I like to tame the garlic by sautéing it with the onion, but if you want that raw sharpness, just press the garlic into the final mixture and stir well. Serve with pita triangles, olives, and tomatoes.

2 medium white eggplants, pierced all over with a skewer
2 tablespoons olive oil, plus additional for oiling the baking sheet
4 cloves garlic
1 medium yellow onion, diced
½ cup tahini (sesame paste)
¼ cup freshly squeezed lemon juice
1 to 2 canned chipotle peppers, chopped, with 2 teaspoons of
   their adobo sauce (optional)
Salt and freshly ground black pepper
½ cup chopped scallions, white and light green parts only
¼ cup toasted pine nuts
½ teaspoon toasted sesame oil, or to taste
Dashes of Tabasco sauce to taste
Minced parsley leaves, for garnish

Heat the oven to 450°F. Place the eggplants on an oiled foil-lined baking sheet flesh side down. Roast for 40 to 45 minutes, until very soft. Let the eggplants cool.

Meanwhile, in a medium skillet, heat 2 tablespoons of olive oil over medium heat. Pass the garlic cloves through a sturdy garlic press into the oil, and immediately add the diced onion. Sauté, stirring, until the onion begins to darken, 15 minutes. Transfer to a roomy bowl.

Scoop out the insides of the eggplants and place the pulp in the bowl with the onion. Add the tahini, lemon juice, chipotle pepper(s), if using, and a judicious amount of salt and pepper. Puree the ingredients to your liking with an immersion blender on medium to medium-low speed. Stir in the scallions, pine nuts, sesame oil, and Tabasco. Mix well. You might want to thin the mixture with a little water. Taste carefully, and add sesame oil, Tabasco, and/or salt as needed. Garnish with the minced parsley, and serve at room temperature.

Yield: varies, but surely enough for 4 appetizers

Deviled Eggs

These beloved stuffed eggs have been around for centuries in one form or another, but their name didn't come about until the eighteenth century in England, when "deviling" and "food" were first conjoined in print. Mustard was usually involved, as it is here. Do try to use smoked Spanish paprika. To make peeling the eggs a lot easier, use eggs that are at least a week old, but not so old that they float in water. Those must be tossed. The immersion blender will make your filling fluffier than it's ever been before.

8 hard-boiled large eggs
¼ cup plus 2 tablespoons prepared mayonnaise
1 tablespoon minced fresh herbs, such as chervil, chives, and/or tarragon leaves
1 tablespoon smooth Dijon mustard, or to taste
2 teaspoons champagne or white wine vinegar
¼ teaspoon Worcestershire sauce
¼ teaspoon Tabasco sauce
¼ teaspoon ground cumin
¼ teaspoon salt
¼ teaspoon freshly ground white pepper
1 teaspoon freshly squeezed lemon juice
Sweet smoked Spanish paprika, for garnish
Bottled pickled sliced jalapeño peppers, for garnish (optional)

Shell the eggs, halve them lengthwise, and carefully remove the yolk halves, leaving the white halves intact.

In a large bowl, combine the mayonnaise, herbs, mustard, vinegar, Worcestershire and Tabasco sauces, cumin, salt, white pepper, and lemon juice. Blend the mixture with an immersion blender until well combined, fluffy, and soft.

Either spoon the mixture in mounds into the egg white cavities, or pipe the mixture into the egg whites with a pastry bag fitted with a star tip, or transfer the mixture to a plastic storage bag, snip off a lower corner of the bag, and pipe the egg yolk mixture into the egg whites. Finish with a gentle sprinkling of paprika and a pickled jalapeño slice, if desired.

Yield: 16 deviled eggs

Cheddar Beer Dip

The 1960s wouldn't have been the 1960s without this dip, although then it was most often made with processed cheese, such as Velveeta or—God help us—Cheez Whiz. You have a lot of control over the texture, so if you like your dip chunky, restrain your immersion blender.

16 ounces (1 pound) sharp Cheddar cheese, freshly grated
1 cup beer
2 scallions, white and light green parts only, minced
1 teaspoon bittersweet smoked Spanish paprika
½ teaspoon dry mustard
½ to 1 teaspoon garlic powder, or to taste, or 2 cloves garlic, pressed
Shakes of Tabasco sauce to taste

Place the cheese and beer in a large bowl. With an immersion blender on medium-high speed, puree the mixture. Add the scallions, paprika, mustard, garlic, and Tabasco. Puree the mixture again. Refrigerate the dip, covered, for ½ hour—no longer—to let the flavors meld. Serve with good crackers, potato chips, tortilla chips, crudités, gherkins, and/or toast points.

Yield: 3 cups

Horseradish Cheese Dip

Do make the effort to find fresh horseradish. It's actually quite easy to grow, but if you haven't planned that far in advance you can also find it in most gourmet food shops.

½ pound cottage cheese, or fresh ricotta cheese
4 ounces cream cheese, softened watchfully in a microwave
  oven, 10 to 15 seconds on high, depending on your oven's
  wattage
1 tablespoon freshly grated peeled horseradish
1 teaspoon freshly grated ginger
1 teaspoon smooth Dijon mustard
½ teaspoon bittersweet smoked Spanish paprika
½ teaspoon Tabasco sauce
½ teaspoon salt
½ teaspoon freshly ground white pepper
½ teaspoon dried imported oregano, or 1 teaspoon fresh
  oregano leaves, minced
½ teaspoon dried powdered sage
1 teaspoon fresh thyme leaves

In a medium bowl, blend all the ingredients thoroughly with an immersion blender. Stir and blend again, then refrigerate for a few hours to let the flavors meld. Serve at room temperature with crudités, crackers, and/or chips. This recipe keeps, covered tightly, 4 to 5 days.

Yield: about 2 cups

Pesto Dip

Basil is the very distillation of summer itself. The leaves taste like raw sunshine. In July and August, when there's so much basil here in the northeast, I make quarts of pesto and freeze it without adding the Parmigiano-Reggiano cheese, in tightly covered 1-cup containers. It thaws fairly quickly, and then I can add the cheese and use it on pasta or drizzled into salads with a splash of balsamic vinegar for the taste and scent of summer all winter long.

This is an excellent example of an immersion blender recipe that saves lots of time and dirty dishes. You're sullying only 2 bowls (one for serving), a spoon or whisk, a cheese grater, and the tip of the immersion blender.

This dip works well with all kinds of crudités. Use your imagination, but don't omit red bell pepper strips, cucumber spears, and pita triangles.

3 cups tightly packed fresh basil leaves
¾ cup extra virgin olive oil
¼ cup plus 1 tablespoon pine nuts, toasted if you wish
3 cloves garlic, pressed at the last minute
¾ cup freshly grated Parmigiano-Reggiano, or slightly more to taste
Salt to taste
1 cup crème fraîche
½ cup prepared mayonnaise
⅓ cup buttermilk, plus more to thin the dip if necessary

To make the pesto: Place the basil, olive oil, pine nuts, and garlic in a large bowl. Pulse with the immersion blender until you have a creamy mixture, stirring often. (If you're going to freeze the extra cup of pesto, do so now.) Stir in the cheese and blend the mixture well. You could give it another buzz or two with the blender. Season with salt to taste.

Make the dip: Measure out 2 cups of the pesto and place it in a serving bowl. Refrigerate the remaining pesto (or see the headnote for freezing instructions). Add the crème fraîche, mayonnaise, and buttermilk to the pesto and blend well with the immersion blender. Thin the dip with a little additional buttermilk if you think it's too stiff.

Use the dip at once or freeze in increments as discussed in the headnote.

Finished pesto will keep, tightly covered, in the refrigerator for up to 1 week.

Yield: about 3 cups

DRINKS

Tom and Jerry

This is a warmed and warming version of eggnog that originated in London in the early nineteenth century, and quickly became a holiday tradition. It's time it was revived!

2 large eggs
2 tablespoons sugar
2 ounces dark rum, such as Myers's
½ to 1 cup good bourbon such as Jim Beam
¼ teaspoon ground cinnamon
⅛ teaspoon ground cloves
1½ cups very hot but not boiling whole milk

In a large heatproof pitcher, blend the eggs with the sugar, rum, bourbon, cinnamon, and cloves with an immersion blender. With your free hand, pour the very hot milk into the pitcher in a steady stream with the blender running. Mix well and serve at once in heated mugs.

Yield: 4 drinks

Bloody Marys with Three Peppers

Certainly not for sissies!

2½ cups chilled vodka
½ cup chopped onion
2 small cloves garlic, pressed
2 small jalapeños, stemmed, seeded, and coarsely chopped
1 habanero or Scotch bonnet pepper, stemmed, seeded, and
  coarsely chopped
1 medium red bell pepper, stemmed, seeded, and coarsely
  chopped
2 tablespoons freshly squeezed lemon juice
5 cups tomato or V8 juice
3 tablespoons freshly grated horseradish
2 teaspoons celery salt
1 teaspoon freshly ground black pepper
Lime wedges and celery ribs, for serving

In a 1-quart glass measure, combine the vodka with the onion,
garlic, jalapeños, habanero, bell pepper, and lemon juice. With
an immersion blender, puree the mixture until smooth.

In a large pitcher (at least ½ gallon), combine the vodka mixture with the tomato juice, horseradish, celery salt, and pepper
and stir vigorously to blend. Strain the mixture into ice-filled tall
glasses and serve with the lime wedges and celery ribs.

Yield: 6 to 8 drinks

Papaya-Mango Smoothie

I think tropical ingredients work best in smoothies. You can use sweetened coconut milk, such as Coco Lopez, but then you'd want rum . . .

1 ripe papaya, peeled, seeded, and sliced
1 ripe mango, peeled, pitted, and sliced
1 cup half-and-half or whole milk
1 cup water
2 tablespoons sugar
1 teaspoon vanilla extract
Mint sprigs, for garnish

Place all the ingredients in a 1-quart glass measure. Pulse the immersion blender with an up-and-down motion below the surface of the ingredients until the mixture is smooth. Serve the smoothies in chilled glasses and garnish with mint sprigs.

Yield: 2 servings

Orange Buttermilk-Yogurt Smoothie

I use superfine sugar almost exclusively. You can make your own from regular granulated sugar by pulsing it in a food processor until it's fine and almost powdery.

¾ cup freshly squeezed orange juice
Finely grated zest of 1 orange
2 teaspoons freshly grated ginger
1 tablespoon superfine sugar
1 cup buttermilk
8 ounces whole milk plain yogurt
¼ cup Grand Marnier, or to taste

Combine all the ingredients in a large pitcher. Blend them well with an immersion blender, and make the mixture foamy by blending for 45 seconds on high, with the blender just under the surface of the liquid, to incorporate as much air as possible.

Yield: 2 to 3 drinks

Green Lizard

The poor man's version of this exotic drink uses a can of frozen condensed Minute Maid limeade, 1 cup of rum, and macerated mint. But this version is much better.

1 bunch mint, leaves only
¾ cup freshly squeezed lime juice
¼ cup simple syrup (see below)
¾ to 1 cup white rum, or to desired level of toxicity

Combine all the ingredients in a large pitcher. Blend them with an immersion blender until well combined and the mint appears as little green flecks in the mixture. Serve over ice.

To make simple syrup, use two parts sugar to one part water. Bring the water to a boil, stir in the sugar, turn off the heat, and stir until the sugar is completely dissolved. Let the syrup cool completely.

Yield: 4 servings

Honeydew Melon Milk Shake

This is highly refreshing. You can leave out the Cointreau, but I wouldn't.

1 ripe medium honeydew melon, peeled, seeded, and coarsely
    chopped
1 cup milk
1 teaspoon freshly grated ginger
1 tablespoon freshly squeezed lemon juice
1 tablespoon honey
2 tablespoons Cointreau
1 pint vanilla ice cream, slightly softened
Mint sprigs, for garnish

Place the melon and milk in a large pitcher. Puree the mixture with the immersion blender. Add the ginger, lemon juice, honey, and Cointreau and puree again until smooth. Add the ice cream in large spoonfuls and puree the mixture once more. Divide it among 4 glasses and serve the shakes garnished with the mint sprigs.

Yield: 4 servings

SOUPS

Clam and Corn Chowder

The only real Spanish chorizo currently available (that is, currently allowed) in the United States is Palacios. Portuguese sausage (linguiça) or Polish kielbasa can be substituted, but chorizo is best here because it releases its deep flavors and colors as it cooks. If you want your chowder to have a clammier flavor, substitute bottled clam juice for the chicken broth. I just find that too often bottled clam juice is funky.

2 tablespoons olive oil
8 ounces hard Spanish chorizo, preferably Palacios, hot or sweet (see headnote), sliced into ⅛-inch-thin coins
1 large white onion, coarsely chopped
1 cup dry white vermouth
1½ cups heavy cream
3 dozen littleneck clams, scrubbed
1 cup corn kernels, cut from 2 to 3 ears, cob scraped with the back of the knife to yield the juices
1 medium leek, white and tender green parts only, thoroughly rinsed and coarsely chopped
1 small celery rib, cut into ¼-inch dice
1 medium carrot, peeled and cut into ¼-inch dice
2 medium Jersey beefsteak tomatoes, peeled, halved, seeded, squeezed, and roughly diced
2 thyme sprigs
1 teaspoon ground coriander
1 tablespoon all-purpose flour
2 cups chicken broth
¾ pound Yukon gold potatoes, peeled and sliced into ½-inch dice

1 cup milk
Salt and freshly ground black pepper
Snipped chives, for garnish

Heat 1 tablespoon olive oil in a stainless-steel 12-inch skillet. Add the chorizo and cook it over moderately low heat until the fat is rendered, stirring often, about 4 minutes.

Add the onion and cook, stirring occasionally, until softened, about 7 minutes.

Add ½ cup of the vermouth and boil the mixture over moderately high heat until evaporated, about 7 minutes.

Add 1 cup of the heavy cream and bring to a boil. Add the clams, cover, and cook until they begin to open, about 2 minutes. As the clams open, transfer them to a large bowl. Remove the skillet from the heat.

Pull the clams from their shells, discard the shells, and return the clams to the bowl. Pour the cream mixture over the clams and set aside.

In a large saucepan, heat the remaining 1 tablespoon of olive oil. Add the corn, leek, celery, carrot, tomatoes, thyme, and coriander. Cover and cook over low heat, stirring occasionally, until the vegetables soften, about 10 minutes.

Add the remaining ½ cup of vermouth and simmer it over moderately high heat until evaporated, about 4 minutes.

Add the flour and cook, stirring, for 1 minute. Gradually stir in the chicken broth and bring to a boil over moderately high heat, stirring constantly. Reduce the heat to low, cover, and simmer for 5 minutes. Puree the soup with an immersion blender.

In a medium saucepan, cover the potatoes with water and bring them to a boil. Cook until just tender, about 5 minutes. Drain the potatoes and add them to the soup, along with the milk and the remaining ½ cup of heavy cream.

Bring the soup to a gentle simmer over low heat. Stir the reserved clams into the cream and heat until just warmed through. Season the soup to taste with salt and pepper and serve it right away, sprinkled with the snipped chives.

Yield: 8 servings

Cream of Cauliflower Soup

White truffle oil and Stilton cheese make this soup almost shockingly good. Here, the immersion blender transforms cooked rice to a soup thickener. You could even omit the cream, but what fun would that be? Buy truffle oil at any gourmet food shop in a small quantity, and keep it refrigerated after you open it. The oil can turn rancid fairly quickly, so use it up within a few weeks. Suffer!

4 tablespoons unsalted butter
3 large or 6 small leeks, white parts only, thoroughly rinsed and
    sliced
2 large russet potatoes, peeled and roughly chopped
2 celery stalks, chopped
4 cups chicken stock
1 medium cauliflower, florets only
¼ cup crumbled Stilton cheese
1 cup heavy cream
1 cup cooked rice
Salt and freshly ground black pepper
Pinch of freshly grated nutmeg
½ teaspoon white truffle oil (optional)

Melt the butter in a large saucepan and sweat the leeks, potatoes, and celery for 15 minutes, covered, over gentle heat, stirring every few minutes.

   Pour the stock over the mixture and add the cauliflower. Bring to a boil and cook until the vegetables are tender, about 20 minutes. Stir in the Stilton cheese and simmer for 3 minutes. Let the mixture cool slightly. Add the cream and rice. Thoroughly puree the soup with an immersion blender. Season with the salt and pepper and nutmeg. Stir in the (very nice) white truffle oil, if desired.

Serve the soup with piping hot garlic bread dribbled with a little more truffle oil.

Yield: about 4 servings

Roasted Yellow Pepper Soup

This soup is as beautiful as it is delicious.

  2 large yellow bell peppers
  1 tablespoon unsalted butter
  1 tablespoon canola oil
  1 medium leek, white and light green parts only, thoroughly
     rinsed and thinly sliced
  1 large Yukon gold potato, peeled and cut into ½-inch cubes
  4 cups chicken broth, low sodium if canned
  6 threads saffron, crumbled
  1 teaspoon kosher salt
  1 cup canned diced tomatoes, drained, preferably Muir Glen
  1 teaspoon orange zest, finely minced
  Salt and freshly ground white pepper to taste
  Crumbled fresh goat cheese, preferably with green peppercorns
     or caraway seeds, for serving

Over a burner flame or under a hot broiler, roast the yellow peppers, turning often, until they're blackened and blistered all over. Place the peppers in a plastic bag and let them steam for 15 minutes. Rub off the skins with paper towels and seed and stem the peppers; do not rinse. Roughly chop the peppers and set them aside.

In a large saucepan, melt the butter in the canola oil over medium heat. Add the leek and sauté, stirring, for 5 minutes. Add the potato cubes, stir for 1 minute, then pour in the chicken broth and add the saffron, salt, and tomatoes. Raise the heat and bring it to a boil, then lower the heat and simmer for 15 minutes. Add the chopped yellow peppers and simmer for 5 minutes longer.

Puree the mixture with an immersion blender until very smooth. Stir in the orange zest and salt and white pepper. Serve the soup hot, sprinkled with the crumbled goat cheese.

Yield: 4 servings

Roasted Kabocha Squash Soup

A rich, shapely cousin of the mighty pumpkin, kabocha squash is well worth seeking out. It has the same shape as a pumpkin, but has a harder dark green outer skin and thicker orange flesh with a natural earthy sweetness. When roasted, the flesh softens to the texture of a baked potato, and the flavor deepens. The freshly brewed green tea also gives a certain depth to the proceedings. Kabocha squash is available year-round. Look for one with a firm, smooth outer skin and an intact stem that isn't too dried out. If you just can't find kabocha, you can substitute butternut squash or sugar pumpkin, but. . . .

One 4-pound kabocha squash, halved lengthwise and seeded
3 tablespoons canola oil
¼ pound thickly sliced bacon, cut into ¼-inch pieces
4 large shallots, minced
1 Granny Smith apple, peeled, cored, and sliced into ½-inch
   pieces
1 tablespoon fresh marjoram leaves or 2 teaspoons fresh
   oregano leaves
1 teaspoon finely grated ginger or ½ teaspoon powdered ginger
1 tablespoon dark maple syrup or honey
¼ teaspoon freshly grated nutmeg
3 cups chicken broth
2 cups freshly brewed green tea
1 cup crème fraîche
1 tablespoon cider vinegar
Salt and freshly ground black pepper

Set a rack in the middle of the oven and preheat to 400°F. Prick the skin of the halved and seeded squash with the tines of a fork or a trussing needle. Rub the squash all over with 2 tablespoons of the canola oil and place it on a parchment-lined roasting pan. Roast the squash until tender, 50 to 60 minutes. Let it cool, then scrape out the flesh, chop it roughly, and set aside.

In a large 3- to 4-quart stockpot, cook the bacon over medium heat, stirring occasionally, until nicely browned. With a slotted spoon, transfer the bacon to paper towels and set it aside.

Add the remaining tablespoon of canola oil to the bacon fat in the pot, then add the shallots, apple pieces, and marjoram or oregano. Lower the heat to medium low and cook the mixture slowly, stirring occasionally, until the apple is fairly tender, about 10 minutes.

Stir in the ginger, syrup, and nutmeg, then add the squash. Pour in the chicken broth and green tea. Bring the mixture to a boil, then lower the heat and simmer for 15 minutes. Turn off the heat and stir in the crème fraîche and cider vinegar.

Puree the soup with an immersion blender until very smooth. If the soup seems too thick, add up to a cup more water or broth. Taste the soup carefully, and add salt and pepper as needed.

Serve the soup piping hot, scattered with the reserved bacon.

Yield: 6 servings

Spicy Tomato Shrimp Soup

This unusual soup is another "dream" recipe. I'm very fond of spicy soups, and the way this is prepared, the shrimp doesn't overcook, as is usually the case. One downside: This soup isn't particularly re-heatable.

5 cloves garlic, unpeeled
2 to 3 habanero peppers, stemmed and seeded
8 tablespoons (1 stick) unsalted butter, cut into 8 pieces
½ teaspoon cinnamon, freshly ground if possible
¼ cup minced shallots
Two 28-ounce cans diced tomatoes in juice, not tomato puree
    (Muir Glen organic "fire-roasted" is perfect)
3 anchovies, chopped
6 saffron threads
1 cup heavy cream
1 cup evaporated milk
1 cup chicken stock
Salt and freshly ground black pepper to taste
1 pound rock shrimp, or medium shrimp, peeled and deveined
Freshly chopped flat parsley leaves, for garnish

Preheat the oven to 350°F. Place the garlic and habanero peppers on a 6-inch square of heavy-duty foil. Add 2 tablespoons of the butter, and the cinnamon. To grind the cinnamon sticks, you'll need an electric spice grinder—a cheap coffee bean grinder is ideal. Break the cinnamon sticks into the smallest pieces possible and grind them to powder. Close the foil into a packet and roast for 25 minutes. Let cool, then, reserving all the juices, peel the garlic and snip the habaneros into 6 pieces with scissors.

Meanwhile, in a large saucepan, melt the remaining 6 tablespoons butter over medium heat. Add the shallots and sauté for 5 minutes, or until they are soft. Add the tomatoes with their juice, the anchovies, and saffron. Bring the mixture to a boil, then lower the heat, and simmer for 10 minutes.

Add the garlic and habaneros with their juices, the cream, evaporated milk, and chicken stock and return to a boil, then lower the heat and simmer the soup for 5 minutes. Puree the soup thoroughly with an immersion blender. Taste it carefully and season with salt and pepper.

Raise the heat. Add the shrimp, bring to a boil, turn off the heat, and serve the soup at once, scattering each serving with the parsley.

Yield: 6 servings

Cream of Wild Mushroom Soup with Gruyère Croutons

This special-occasion soup is endlessly buttery and creamy.

1 stick unsalted butter, softened
1 cup sliced fennel bulb
1 cup sliced celery stalks
1 cup sliced shallots
½ cup sliced carrots
½ cup chopped onions
4 medium cloves garlic, pressed
4 cups sliced shiitake mushroom caps (about 8 ounces)
3 cups sliced crimini mushrooms (about 6 ounces)
2 cups sliced oyster mushrooms (about 3 ounces)
½ cup dry white vermouth
¼ cup Madeira wine
¼ cup Wondra flour
½ teaspoon freshly grated nutmeg
2 quarts low-sodium chicken stock, preferably homemade
¾ cup heavy cream
Salt and freshly ground black pepper
6 square slices or 3 oblong slices pumpernickel bread
1 cup grated Gruyère cheese
Sour cream, for garnish

Melt 6 tablespoons of the butter in a large soup kettle over medium heat. Add the fennel, celery, shallots, carrots, onions, and garlic and sauté the vegetables, stirring, until they begin to soften, about 10 minutes. Add the mushrooms and sauté, stirring, until they begin to release their juices, about 5 minutes. Pour in the vermouth and Madeira and raise the heat to medium-high. Bring the mixture to a boil and cook, stirring often, until the liquid thickens into a glaze, about 6 minutes.

With a fork or your fingers, mix the remaining 2 tablespoons of soft butter with the flour in a small bowl until a smooth paste forms. Add the flour paste to the mushroom mixture in the pot and stir until the paste melts and the mixture coats the vegetables. Grate in the nutmeg and gradually stir in the chicken stock. Bring to a boil, stirring frequently. Reduce the heat to medium-low and simmer until the mushrooms are tender, stirring often, about 10 minutes. Stir in the cream. Season carefully with salt and pepper.

Preheat the oven to 375°F. Place the pumpernickel slices on a baking sheet and toast them for 10 minutes. Scatter the Gruyère evenly over the bread and toast for another 5 minutes. When slightly cooled, cut the bread into 1-inch croutons with scissors.

Using an immersion blender, puree the soup until smooth and creamy. Serve the soup piping hot in wide bowls with several croutons and a dollop of sour cream on each serving.

Yield: 10 servings

Avgolemono Soup
(Lemon Chicken Egg Drop Soup)

This soup does not reheat, so I've adapted the recipe for 2 servings. It doubles nicely. Don't be tempted to use canned broth for this: You need a certain thickness that only homemade gelatinous chicken stock can provide. Add the rice to the broth in the same hour you plan to serve the soup. So make your favorite chicken stock, and reduce it by one-quarter to concentrate the flavors. Lightly puree the final mixture; you want about half the rice to be whole.

4 cups homemade chicken stock, reduced to 3 cups
½ cup basmati rice
2 large eggs
¼ cup fresh lemon juice, plus 1 tablespoon, if needed, from 1 large lemon
Salt and freshly ground black pepper
Snippets of fresh dill (optional)

Bring the reduced stock to a boil and add the rice. Reduce the heat to a simmer, cover, and let the rice cook until tender, about 20 minutes. Turn off the heat.

Whisk the eggs and lemon juice in a medium heatproof bowl just to combine. Whisk 2 tablespoons of the hot broth into the mixture, then 2 more, then 2 more. To prevent curdling, stir the mixture into the hot (but *not* boiling) soup gradually, while stirring constantly. Partially puree the soup with an immersion blender, until about half the rice is pureed, to thicken the soup.

Season the soup to taste with salt and pepper and perhaps another tablespoon of lemon juice and serve it at once, sprinkled with dill, if desired.

Yield: 2 servings

Cream of Tomato and Fennel Soup

This soothing, rich soup with its pronounced anise accents makes a very fine lunch, served with fresh warm bread and followed by Gorgonzola cheese and fruit.

1 stick unsalted butter (plus 2 tablespoons to finish)
2 medium fennel bulbs, top fronds removed, tough outer leaves discarded, bulbs cored and coarsely chopped
10 to 12 medium-large shallots, peeled and well chopped
8 cloves garlic, minced
Two 28-ounce cans diced tomatoes (Muir Glen preferred), with their liquid, or 6 medium-large dead-ripe tomatoes, peeled and seeded
Kosher salt and freshly ground black pepper to taste
1½ cups unsalted chicken broth, preferably homemade
2 to 3 tablespoons Pernod (optional)
1½ cups heavy cream or half-and-half
Crème fraîche, for garnish

Melt the stick of butter in a large soup kettle. Sweat the fennel, shallots, and garlic over medium-low heat until quite limp, covered, for 15 minutes, stirring every few minutes to avoid browning. Then sauté for 10 minutes uncovered, stirring often.

Add the tomatoes and their liquid. Simmer the mixture very gently, uncovered, for 30 minutes.

Add salt and pepper, cool slightly, and puree the mixture using an immersion blender.

Add the chicken broth, Pernod, if using, and cream. Bring the mixture just to a boil. Stir in the remaining 2 tablespoons of butter.

Serve with a good dollop of crème fraîche.

Yield: 6 to 8 servings

Curried Pumpkin Soup with Toasted Pumpkin Seeds

This soup is Halloween in a bowl.

1 pumpkin, 4 to 5 pounds
2 tablespoons olive oil
1 tablespoon unsalted butter
½ cup finely chopped shallots
5 cups chicken broth, low salt if canned
1 medium russet potato, peeled and chopped into ½-inch
  chunks
1 large carrot, peeled and sliced crosswise into ½-inch pieces
1 tablespoon dark brown sugar
2 teaspoons molasses
Finely minced zest of 1 orange
2 teaspoons Madras curry powder
1 cup heavy cream
Dash of Tabasco sauce
Salt and freshly ground black pepper to taste
½ teaspoon freshly grated nutmeg
1½ cups grated sharp Cheddar cheese
Toasted pumpkin seeds (recipe follows)

Cut the pumpkin in half and scoop out the seeds and strings. Reserve the seeds. Cut away the hard peel with a paring knife or vegetable peeler and chop the flesh. You should have about 6 cups of pumpkin flesh.

In a large saucepan over medium-low heat, warm the olive oil with the butter. When the butter has melted, add the shallots and sauté them, stirring occasionally, until they're translucent, 3 to 4 minutes. Add the broth, pumpkin, potato, and carrot, raise the heat to high, and bring the mixture to a boil. Reduce the heat to low, cover, and simmer until the vegetables are tender, 20 to 25 minutes.

Puree the soup with an immersion blender until very smooth. Stir in the brown sugar, molasses, orange zest, and curry powder. Over low heat, stir in the cream and Tabasco. Taste the soup carefully. Season with salt and pepper and add the grated nutmeg.

Ladle the soup into warmed bowls and, at the table, pass the Cheddar cheese and pumpkin seeds for sprinkling.

Yield: 6 servings

Toasted Pumpkin Seeds (Pepitas)

Preheat the oven to 250°F. Remove the seeds from the pumpkin(s) and pull as much of the strands and pulp away from them as you can. However, don't rinse the seeds.

In a roomy bowl, stir the seeds with clarified butter, peanut oil, or canola oil, about ½ cup of fat for every 4 cups of seeds. Add a nominal amount of kosher salt. Try adding a bit of thyme, oregano, cumin, coriander, cardamom, and/or cayenne, if you like.

Line baking sheet(s) with parchment paper or Silpat mats. Spread the seeds in one layer on the sheets. Toast them slowly for about an hour, checking them every 10 to 15 minutes and stirring if they're browning unevenly.

Store the toasted seeds in tightly sealed containers lined with paper towels. They'll keep for about 1 month. If they get soggy, re-toast them in a 200-degree oven, stirring every 5 minutes, for 15–20 minutes.

SALADS, DRESSINGS, AND SAUCES

Faux Caesar Salad with Roasted Garlic–Chipotle Dressing

This recipe circumvents concerns about eating raw eggs by using store-bought mayonnaise, for which the eggs are pasteurized. There are a number of unconventional ingredients, but the traditional anchovies manage to ground the flavors. Quartered hard-boiled eggs are included among the salad ingredients; you can just as easily nest a warm poached egg on top of the romaine just before you drizzle on the dressing with the squeeze bottle. The dressing itself keeps at least 3 days, refrigerated, right in the squeeze bottle; you'll be justifiably tempted to apply the dressing to grilled steak or fish or soft fried eggs.

For The Dressing
    4 large garlic heads, separated into cloves, left unpeeled
    ½ cup mayonnaise
    2 tablespoons smooth Dijon mustard
    3 to 4 anchovies, soaked for 20 minutes in milk, chopped
    ⅓ cup freshly grated Parmigiano-Reggiano cheese
    3 chipotle peppers, canned with adobo sauce (more or less, to taste, but watch that sauce—it's hot!)
    2 tablespoons balsamic vinegar
    1 tablespoon good red wine vinegar
    1 tablespoon fresh lemon juice
    Plenty of freshly and finely ground black pepper
    ⅓ cup olive oil
    ⅓ cup peanut oil

Wrap the garlic cloves in foil and roast them for ½ hour at 400°F. Let the cloves cool. Squeeze the pulp into a cylindrical container slightly larger in circumference than your immersion blender. Add the mayonnaise, mustard, anchovies, cheese, chipotle peppers, balsamic and red wine vinegars, lemon juice, and pepper to taste. Puree well with the immersion blender. Add the olive and peanut oils and emulsify with the immersion blender. Taste the mixture for heat and add another chipotle if you wish, pureeing again. If you want to be de rigueur, transfer the dressing to a squeeze bottle with a medium tip. Otherwise, just set the dressing aside.

For the Croutons
    One 14- to 16-ounce crusty loaf of French or Italian peasant
        bread
    4 tablespoons melted unsalted butter
    4 tablespoons extra virgin olive oil
    1 teaspoon kosher salt
    Several dashes of Tabasco sauce
    ½ teaspoon freshly ground black pepper

Preheat the oven to 450°F. Remove the crusts from the loaf and cut into ¾-inch cubes.

In a very large bowl, combine the butter and oil. Add the bread cubes and toss with your hands until the cubes are well coated. Add the salt, Tabasco, and pepper and toss again. Spread the cubes on a foil-lined baking sheet large enough to hold them in one layer. Bake them for about 10 minutes, until just browned. (Don't bother to rinse the bowl.)

For the Salad
2 romaine lettuce hearts, outer dark leaves removed, cut into
    1- to 2-inch pieces
Plenty of freshly grated Parmigiano-Reggiano cheese
¼ cup red wine vinegar

To Assemble the Salad
3 to 4 quartered hard-cooked eggs, or 1 poached egg per
    person

In the crouton bowl, toss the romaine lettuce with the cheese and enough of the red wine vinegar to make the leaves glisten. Squirt in about ½ cup of the dressing, and toss the salad with the croutons. Divide the salad among 4 plates, top with the eggs, and decoratively drizzle a bit more dressing over all.

Yield: 4 servings

Green Goddess Dressing

This dressing was all the rage in the 1920s, when it was developed at the Palm Court Restaurant in San Francisco, and named for a George Arliss theatrical vehicle called The Green Goddess. *(Arliss stayed at the Palace Hotel, which housed the Palm Court.) I've tweaked, nipped, and tucked the original and adapted it for the immersion blender.*

The dressing should rest for at least 3 hours, refrigerated, to bring its flavors together. This recipe makes about 2½ cups of dressing, but it will keep, tightly covered, for about 5 days. In addition to dressing a mixture of romaine, Boston lettuce, and chicory, it makes a nice dip for crudités. It should be served fairly cold. Use the dressing as soon as possible, because it tends to darken unattractively over time.

1 cup mayonnaise
1 cup sour cream
2 very fresh large egg yolks
½ cup flat parsley leaves
2 tablespoons tarragon or chervil leaves
1 large scallion, white and light green parts only, chopped, about
    1 tablespoon
3 to 4 anchovy fillets, soaked in milk for 10 minutes, then rinsed,
    drained, and chopped
2 tablespoons freshly squeezed lime juice, plus 1 teaspoon finely
    grated zest from one lime
½ cup finely chopped chives
Freshly ground black pepper to taste
2 to 3 tablespoons buttermilk, as needed, to thin the dressing

Place the mayonnaise, sour cream, egg yolks, parsley, tarragon, scallion, anchovies, and lime juice in a mixing bowl just large enough to hold everything. Puree the ingredients with an immersion blender until the parsley is finely minced, and the mixture is fairly smooth and pale green. Add the chives, pepper, and enough buttermilk to thin the mixture so you can puree it a bit further. Buzz with the immersion blender until the chives are mixed in well. Taste the salad for seasoning, adding salt if necessary. Use the dressing as soon as you can if you want that lovely pale green color, or if you must hold it, cover tightly, and put it in the refrigerator, where it will keep for 1 to 2 days.

Yield: 2½ cups

Anchovy–Gorgonzola Cheese Salad Dressing

This is not for the faint of heart, but it's substantially delicious. This dresses romaine lettuce hearts to the nines! It also does well on most any hearty tossed salad.

⅔ cup good olive oil
10 anchovy fillets, with a little of their packing oil, chopped well
1 bottled pimiento, drained well and chopped
3 tablespoons champagne vinegar
3 tablespoons freshly squeezed lemon juice
1 clove garlic, pressed through a sturdy press
½ teaspoon sugar
½ teaspoon Dijon mustard
½ teaspoon celery seeds
½ teaspoon Worcestershire sauce
½ teaspoon Tabasco sauce, or to taste
½ teaspoon bittersweet smoked Spanish paprika
½ cup crumbled Gorgonzola cheese

With an immersion blender, blend everything in a large bowl until absolutely smooth. The dressing will keep, tightly covered and refrigerated, for 1 week.

Yield: 1¼ cups

Tomatillo Salsa

For that precious handful of late summer weeks when fresh local tomatillos are available in the Northeast, I make this salsa a few times a week. It freezes very well, so you might want to double the recipe for an instant party later in October. As is, this recipe makes about 3½ cups, which is a lot.

1½ pounds bright green, firm, medium-small tomatillos, husked and rinsed (they're sticky)
1½ cups chopped white onions
1 large green pepper, stemmed, seeded, peeled (if you wish), and chopped into 1-inch pieces
2 jalapeño peppers, stemmed, seeded, and chopped into 1-inch pieces
6 large cloves garlic, peeled and roughly chopped
½ teaspoon orange zest, finely minced
3 to 4 tablespoons peanut oil
2 teaspoons kosher salt
1 teaspoon freshly ground black pepper
Droplets of Tabasco or another favored hot sauce, as needed
½ cup coarsely chopped fresh cilantro leaves and delicate stems

Preheat the oven to 450°F. In a 3-inch-deep, large cast-iron skillet, stir together everything but the cilantro. Make sure everything is well coated with the oil. Roast the mixture in the middle of the oven for 45 minutes, stirring once at half time.

Cool the mixture. Transfer it to a large bowl. Pulse with the immersion blender *just* until it is coarsely blended. Add the cilantro and pulse 3 to 4 times. Taste carefully. You'll probably want to add a bit more salt, and you might want to brighten the salsa with a few shakes of Tabasco or another hot sauce. Pulse a few more times.

Serve the salsa as a dip at room temperature with low-salt tortilla chips. Or dribble the warmed sauce over sautéed chicken breasts, or substitute it for the sauce in the Mexican Casserole (page 114). Or you may just want to drink the stuff, it's so good!

This will keep, covered and chilled, for 3 to 4 days.

Yield: about 3½ cups

Fresh Tomato Aspic

I remember having wonderful smooth aspics at grown-up parties when I was a child. You don't run across them very often these days, and that's a shame. This is a most refreshing late-August/early-September aspic that suspends—literally—the magical flavors of fresh ripe tomatoes. If it's a hot and humid day, you may need to double the gelatin. Silpat cups work very well in this recipe.

1 pound dead-ripe red tomatoes, stemmed, skinned, and
    seeded
2 shallots
¾ cup cold water
1 envelope unflavored gelatin (2¼ teaspoons)
1½ teaspoons salt, or to taste
1 tablespoon freshly squeezed lime juice
A few shakes of Worcestershire sauce
Tabasco sauce to taste
10 basil leaves, sliced into a chiffonade
8 saffron threads, finely chopped
Olive oil, for oiling the ring mold

Stem and slice the tomatoes, and place them in a saucepan. Mince the shallots and add them to the tomatoes. Add ½ cup of the water. Bring the mixture to a boil and simmer it for 10 minutes. Take it off the heat and finely puree the mixture with an immersion blender.

  Soften the gelatin in the remaining ¼ cup of water for 5 minutes, then dissolve the mixture in a small pan over low heat. Add

the gelatin mixture to the tomato juice. Add the salt, lime juice, Worcestershire, Tabasco, basil, and saffron. Blend the mixture well with the immersion blender, then pour the aspic into a lightly oiled ring mold or into 6 lightly oiled ramekins. Chill the aspic for at least 2 hours.

Serve the aspic on a tumble of lightly dressed mesclun, or with a scoop of cottage cheese or thickened Greek yogurt.

Yield: 6 servings

Red Bell Pepper Coulis

This will enliven a poached chicken breast considerably, but it's also wonderful drizzled over many a sautéed fish fillet. Piquillo peppers are wood fire–roasted mild Spanish red peppers that have a real depth of flavor. They're available at www.tienda.com.

1 tablespoon olive oil
2 meaty red bell peppers, stemmed, seeded, and chopped
¼ cup chopped bottled piquillo peppers (optional, but very nice)
3 shallots, chopped
1 clove garlic, pressed
2 anchovies, rinsed
1 tablespoon tomato paste
½ teaspoon powdered ginger
½ cup dry French vermouth
½ cup low-salt chicken broth
½ cup crème fraîche
Salt and freshly ground black pepper to taste

Heat a medium skillet over medium heat. Add the olive oil, then all the peppers, shallots, and garlic. Sauté until the peppers are soft, 8 to 10 minutes. Add the anchovies, tomato paste, and ginger and sauté for 5 minutes. Stir in the vermouth and broth, and simmer it until reduced by half.

Let the mixture cool for a few minutes, then stir in the crème fraîche and puree the mixture with an immersion blender until very smooth. Taste and add salt and pepper as needed. The coulis will keep, tightly covered and refrigerated, for 3 days.

Yield: about 2 cups

Applesauce for Grown-Ups

A mix of apples adds depth to a dish that so often falls flat after a few mouthfuls. So do blueberries, a few extra spices, vanilla, and a jot of Calvados just before serving. As usual, an immersion blender not only saves you time and spares you extended cleanup, cooling, and reheating but it enables you to control the texture of your sauce. If you like chunky applesauce, you'll know just when to stop blending.

3 pounds apples, preferably a mix of Macintosh, Macoun, and
    Winesap, peeled, cored, and sliced just before cooking
¾ cup cider, or slightly more if the apples aren't very juicy
2 tablespoons freshly squeezed lemon juice
1 cup blueberries, frozen are fine
1 large cinnamon stick
½ teaspoon powdered ginger
½ teaspoon ground mace
½ teaspoon freshly grated nutmeg
Sugar, up to ½ cup, or honey, up to ⅓ cup
1 teaspoon Tahitian vanilla extract
Calvados for serving (optional)

Place the apple slices in a large nonreactive saucepan with the cider, lemon juice, blueberries, and cinnamon stick. Cover and simmer over low heat, stirring every few minutes, until the apples are tender, about 20 minutes. Remove and discard the cinnamon stick.

Stir in the ginger, mace, and nutmeg. Puree the mixture to the

desired consistency with an immersion blender and taste for sweetness. Add the sugar or honey as desired and cook over low heat, stirring constantly, until the sugar or honey is well incorporated, about 1 minute. Turn off the heat and stir in the vanilla.

Serve the applesauce warm, at room temperature, or chilled, with a splash of Calvados, if desired.

Yield: 6 servings

MAIN COURSES

Veal Meat Loaf with Dried Apricot Coulis

This is a recipe that actually came to me in a dream, as did a number of recipes in this book. I woke up and scribbled what I could remember in the dark.

This results in a remarkably tender loaf, and, ironically enough, apricots and saffron go together really well. Usually I try to use organic ingredients, but organic dried apricots are brown, while treated apricots have the beautiful color that you want for this sauce.

2 tablespoons unsalted butter
1 medium yellow onion, finely chopped
1 cup heavy cream
¾ teaspoon saffron threads, crumbled
1 cup chicken broth, low sodium if canned
1½ cups dry bread crumbs
1½ pounds ground veal
½ pound ground pork
2 large eggs
2 large egg yolks
½ cup salted and roasted pistachios (optional)
2 teaspoons fresh thyme leaves, roughly chopped
1 tablespoon capers, rinsed thoroughly
Salt and freshly ground black pepper to taste
10 dried apricots, cut into ¼-inch pieces with oiled scissors
½ cup freshly squeezed orange juice
1 tablespoon Cointreau

½ cup Marsala wine
1 teaspoon grated fresh ginger
1 teaspoon finely chopped orange zest

Preheat the oven to 350°F. Heat the butter in a medium skillet over medium heat and sauté the onion just until it begins to take on some color, 8 minutes. Set the mixture aside to cool.

Heat the heavy cream in a small skillet or in a glass measure in a microwave oven just until it simmers. Stir in the saffron and set the mixture aside to cool.

In another small skillet, reduce the chicken broth to ½ cup. Set it aside to cool.

Combine the cooled saffron cream and the reduced broth with the bread crumbs and set aside for 5 minutes. In a large bowl, combine the cooled onion, the veal, pork, eggs, egg yolks, pistachios, if using, thyme leaves, capers, salt and pepper, and the bread crumb mixture. Mix well with your hands. Shape the mixture into a 9 × 4-inch loaf on a large foil-lined baking sheet. Bake until the center of the loaf registers 160°F on a meat thermometer, about 1 hour.

Meanwhile, make the coulis: Place the apricots in a medium saucepan with the orange juice, Cointreau, Marsala, and ½ cup of filtered water. Bring the mixture just to a boil, simmer for 15 minutes, or until the dried apricot bits are flabby-tender, then set aside to cool. When the mixture has cooled, add the ginger and orange zest, tilt the saucepan, and puree the mixture until smooth with an immersion blender. Taste carefully and add water if you think it's needed.

When the meat loaf is done, be sure to let it rest for 10 minutes to allow it to firm up, then carve it into attractive slices. Drizzle the coulis around the slices and serve.

Yield: 6 servings

Chicken Thighs in
Garlic-Tarragon Cream Sauce

Chicken thighs are my favorite chicken piece both to cook with and to eat. Unlike most of the rest of the chicken, particularly white meat, it's virtually impossible to overcook thighs (within reason!), and they bear up well to this high-heat pan roasting, ending up with extremely crispy skin.

10 medium cloves garlic, peeled
1½ cups low-salt chicken broth
½ cup dry white vermouth
1 teaspoon dried tarragon
1 teaspoon kosher salt
½ teaspoon white pepper
8 meaty chicken thighs, about three pounds, rinsed and dried
   thoroughly with paper towels
Kosher salt and freshly ground black pepper
3 tablespoons canola oil
3 tablespoons V.S.O.P. brandy
3 tablespoons unsalted butter
3 tablespoons Wondra flour
½ cup heavy cream
1 tablespoon smooth Dijon mustard
1 teaspoon green peppercorns packed in vinegar (optional)
2 tablespoons minced flat-leaf parsley

In a medium partially covered saucepan, simmer the garlic cloves in the broth and vermouth for 30 minutes, until very tender. Let cool slightly and puree the mixture with an immersion blender. Stir in the tarragon, salt, and white pepper and keep warm, covered.

Preheat the oven to 500°F. Pat the chicken completely dry with paper towels and season with salt and black pepper. In a cast-iron skillet large enough to hold all the chicken in one layer, heat the oil until it shimmers over medium-high heat. Carefully add the chicken thighs skin side down and cook until lightly browned, 5 to 8 minutes. Turn the chicken and cook it for 2 minutes. Turn the pieces skin side down again and roast in the oven for about 20 minutes, or until the juices run clear when the thickest part of a thigh is pierced. Remove the chicken to a platter and tent with foil to keep warm.

Drain the fat from the skillet. Take it off the heat, carefully add the brandy and deglaze the skillet, scraping and stirring to get up all the brown bits. Return the skillet to medium heat. Add the butter. When the foam subsides, add the flour and stir the mixture for 2 minutes, or until the flour just begins to take on some color.

Stir in the warm garlic mixture, cream, mustard, and green peppercorns, if desired. Stir until the mixture begins to thicken noticeably, 5 to 7 minutes. Plate the chicken skin side up and add any juices that have accumulated on the platter to the sauce, stirring patiently. Spoon the sauce around the plated chicken and serve it scattered with the parsley.

Yield: 4 servings

Southwestern Chili

This messes around with plenty of heat, so have lots of sour cream at the ready for gringos.

3 dried ancho chiles, lightly toasted over a gas flame or under a hot broiler

3 dried pasilla chiles, or dried Guajillo peppers, also lightly toasted

3 dried New Mexican chiles, also lightly toasted

3 canned chipotle chiles, stemmed and seeded, with 2 teaspoons of the adobo they're canned with

2 tablespoons corn oil

½ cup chopped white onions

3 cloves garlic, pressed

1 pound beef chuck, cut into ¾-inch cubes, excess fat trimmed

1 pound hot Italian sausage, cut into ¾-inch pieces

1 pound sweet Italian sausage, cut into ¾-inch pieces

1 tablespoon sugar

1 teaspoon salt

1 teaspoon freshly ground black pepper

1 teaspoon dried oregano, Mexican if possible

2 teaspoons hot dry mustard

1 teaspoon lime zest, finely chopped

1 bottle good Mexican beer, such as Corona

1 tablespoon masa harina

¼ cup warm dry vermouth

Good tortilla chips, such as Doritos Hint of Lime

6 scallions, chopped

5 jalapeño peppers, stemmed and chopped

1 pound Monterey Jack cheese, grated

1 cup sour cream

Place the dried chiles in a large heatproof bowl and just cover them with boiling water. Let the chiles stand for 30 minutes, until soft. Stem and seed the peppers, if desired, strain the water they were reconstituted in, return the chiles to the water, add the chipotles, and puree the mixture with an immersion blender. Set the mixture aside.

In a Dutch oven large enough to hold the beef cubes in a single layer without crowding, heat the oil over medium heat. Sauté the onions and garlic in the oil, stirring occasionally, until soft. Raise the heat to medium-high, add the beef, and cook until browned. Transfer the beef to a bowl and keep warm.

Sauté the sausage pieces in the skillet over medium-high heat, stirring after a few minutes. When the sausage is nicely browned, raise the heat to high and stir in the pureed chiles, sugar, salt, pepper, oregano, mustard, lime zest, and beer. Stir the mixture well and bring to a boil, then simmer, partially covered, for 45 minutes. Mix the masa harina with the warm vermouth until smooth. Add the mixture to the chili and cook it for 10 minutes longer to thicken. Serve the chili with the tortilla chips, scallions, jalapeños, grated cheese, and sour cream.

Yield: 8 servings

Beef Tenderloin Steaks
Stuffed with Brie, on a
Cranberry-Balsamic Reduction

This wonderfully rich dish with its lingering flavors comes together very quickly, and makes quite a lasting impression. If you don't have ovenproof serving dishes, this recipe is the perfect excuse to get some!

¼ cup dried cranberries
½ cup dry white vermouth
Four 1½- to 2-inch-thick slices from the tournedo end of beef
    tenderloin
1½ cups all-purpose flour
Salt and freshly ground black pepper
2 tablespoons canola oil
4 tablespoons unsalted butter
3 to 4 large shallots, minced
¼ cup balsamic vinegar
1 teaspoon dark molasses, to broaden the sauce
½ pound of just-ripe Brie cheese, peeled if you like

Preheat the oven to 300°F. Place the dried cranberries in a glass measure with the vermouth. Bring the mixture just to a boil in a microwave oven on high heat, 1 to 2 minutes, depending on your oven's wattage. Set aside.

    Split the fillets crosswise, leaving a ¼-inch "hinge" of meat that enables you to open the fillet like a book. Dry the steaks thoroughly with paper towels. Season the flour well with the salt and pepper, and dredge the steaks in the flour. Work quickly so the flavored steaks don't get gummy.

Place the oil and 2 tablespoons of the butter in a large heavy skillet over medium heat. Sauté the dredged and opened fillets, 2 to 3 minutes per side, or until lightly browned. Place each steak on an ovenproof serving dish. Tent the dish with foil to keep warm.

Toss the minced shallots into the skillet and lower the heat to medium-low. Sauté them for 2 minutes, then add the cran-berry/vermouth mixture, balsamic vinegar, and molasses. Tilt the skillet and carefully puree the mixture with an immersion blender. Reduce the sauce over medium heat for 6 minutes or so while proceeding with the steaks.

Lay slices of Brie across one side of each opened steak, and close the other half over, using toothpicks to fasten the meat to-gether over the cheese. Warm in the oven for 3 to 5 minutes, just until the Brie melts.

Swirl the remaining 2 tablespoons of butter into the sauce. Adjust the seasoning, pour the sauce around the steaks, and serve them at once.

Yield: 4 servings

Hanger Steak with a Buttery Port–Shallot Reduction

Hanger steak, or onglet, *or "butcher's tenderloin," hangs free near a steer's kidneys. It is not the same as skirt steak, though it looks like skirt steak on steroids. It has twice the flavor and texture of tenderloin at less than half the cost, and the fact that it hasn't caught on among American consumers just means all the more for those of us who cherish this cut. Ask your butcher to take out the nerve, and to flatten the meat slightly. If you can't get hanger steak, protest, and resort to boneless rib eye or tenderloin steaks at least an inch thick.*

1 cup tawny port wine
4 tablespoons unsalted butter
½ cup finely chopped shallots
About 2 cups beef broth (low-salt canned is fine)
2 teaspoons fresh minced tarragon, or 1 teaspoon dried
2 teaspoons freshly minced thyme leaves, or 1 teaspoon dried
2 tablespoons balsamic vinegar
2 to 3 tablespoons veal demi-glace, if you've got it lying around; otherwise reduce by two-thirds ½ cup of low-sodium beef broth
1 tablespoon peanut oil
About 1½ pounds hanger steak, trimmed, unnerved, cut into 4 pieces, flattened to taste, salted, peppered, and brought to room temperature between sheets of wax paper
Chopped flat-leaf parsley, for garnish (optional)

In a small nonreactive pan over medium-high heat, reduce the cup of port to ⅓ cup, which will take about 6 minutes.

Melt 2 tablespoons of the butter in a medium saucepan. Over medium heat, toss in the shallots. Sauté, stirring, for about 3 minutes, until just golden. Add the rest of the sauce ingredients, except the remaining 2 tablespoons of butter and the demi-glace, if using. Bring the sauce to a simmer, and reduce slowly. After about 10 minutes, puree the sauce with an immersion blender. When the sauce is reduced to just under 1 cup, about 10 minutes longer, add the reduced port to the sauce and keep warm.

Meanwhile, heat an empty cast-iron skillet for 4 minutes over medium-high heat. Swirl in the peanut oil, and carefully lay in the steaks. Cook 3 to 4 minutes per side for rare. (You may well want the services of a "splatter screen.") Transfer the steaks to plates and tent them with foil to keep warm.

Pour the sauce into the hot skillet and simmer, stirring and scraping with a wooden spoon. Add the remaining 2 tablespoons of butter and the demi-glace and stir the sauce just until melted.

Plate the steaks, pour the sauce over and around them, scatter with the parsley, if desired, and serve. Serve with roasted new potatoes? Definitely.

Yield: sauce for at least 2 servings

Indoor Barbecued Country-Style Ribs

Those of us who cannot indulge in outdoor barbecuing certainly needn't deny ourselves the pleasures that grilling can yield. This is nice, messy, Saturday night fun, though not for company, unless you enjoy seeing your friends with barbecue sauce all over their faces. Speaking of that sauce, there will be plenty, so divide it and use some for the marinade and some for basting the ribs at the very end of their indoor barbecuing.

For the Sauce
    8 dried apricots
    ½ cup Kentucky bourbon, possibly a bit more
    1 tablespoon canola oil
    1 medium onion, finely chopped
    2 cloves garlic, pressed
    ⅔ cup canned diced tomatoes with their juices, Muir Glen preferred
    ½ cup packed dark brown sugar
    ¼ cup cider vinegar
    ¼ cup dark molasses (not blackstrap)
    1 tablespoon Worcestershire sauce
    2 teaspoons Dijon mustard, Maille preferred
    1 teaspoon hot smoked Spanish paprika
    ½ teaspoon freshly ground black pepper, plus more as needed
    ½ teaspoon Tabasco sauce, or more to taste
    2 canned chipotle peppers, stemmed and seeded

For the Ribs
2½ to 3 pounds country-style pork ribs, separated into single ribs
Salt and freshly ground black pepper

Make the sauce: Place the dried apricots in a 1-cup glass measure and pour the bourbon over them, ½ cup or to cover. Bring the mixture nearly to a boil in a microwave oven, 1½ to 3 minutes, depending on your oven's wattage. Set the mixture aside for 20 minutes.

In a medium saucepan, heat the oil over medium heat. Add the onion and garlic and cook, stirring often, until the onion takes on some color, about 10 minutes. Add the remaining sauce ingredients, including the apricots and bourbon, and bring the mixture to a simmer. Puree the mixture with an immersion blender. Cook, stirring often, until the sauce is very thick and reduced to about 1 cup, about 15 minutes. Divide the sauce, using two-thirds of it for the marinade and the rest for brushing the ribs at the end of their grilling.

Heat an electric grill to high heat or set a grill pan over medium-high heat for 10 minutes. Season both sides of the ribs with salt and pepper.

Cook the ribs until they are no longer pink at the bone, about

20 minutes, turning them halfway through the cooking time. Brush the reserved barbecue sauce on one side of the ribs, turn them sauce side down, and grill them for a few minutes more until they brown nicely. Brush the unsauced sides, turn the ribs again, and brown them for a few minutes longer.

Yield: 2 large servings

Braised Short Ribs
with Dried Cranberries

Here's a rich and festive recipe in which an immersion blender is indispensable at two stages for creating a silky smooth gravy that incorporates long-braised garlic and shallots.

    2 tablespoons olive oil
    4 pounds beef short ribs, cut between ribs into 2-inch lengths
    Salt and freshly ground black pepper
    2 cups Rioja wine—nothing under $10
    ⅓ cup Wondra flour
    2 cups water
    2 cups low-salt chicken stock
    2 teaspoons balsamic vinegar, if needed
    12 cloves garlic, peeled
    12 large shallots, peeled
    1 teaspoon sea salt
    1 cup dried cranberries (about ¼ pound)
    1 pound gnocchi, your own, or cooked according to package
        directions

In a large enameled cast-iron Dutch oven, heat the oil over medium-high heat. Season the ribs liberally on both sides with salt and pepper. When the oil is just smoking, lay in the ribs and brown them thoroughly on both meaty sides in two batches; don't crowd the pan, or the ribs will steam instead of browning nicely.

Discard the oil, but leave the browned bits. Add the wine to the pan and boil the ribs for about 15 minutes, scraping and stirring occasionally, until the wine is reduced to about ⅓ cup. Measure the wine, return it to the pan, and slowly add an equal amount of flour to make a paste. Gradually whisk in the water, then pour in the stock. Warm the mixture, then puree until velvety with an immersion blender. A few teaspoons of balsamic vinegar may be required to even out the flavors.

Return the ribs to the casserole with any accumulated juices. Add the garlic and shallots and bring to a simmer. Add the sea salt, cover partially, and simmer the ribs over very gentle heat for 2 hours, keeping the sauce just at a slow bubble.

Scatter the cranberries over the meat, stir them in, and continue simmering until the meat is so tender it's practically falling off the bones, about 30 minutes longer. Using a slotted spoon, transfer the ribs, garlic cloves, shallots, and cranberries to a platter. Return the garlic cloves and shallots to the sauce. Skim off any fat, then simmer the sauce over moderate heat to concentrate the flavors, about 5 minutes. Puree again with the immersion blender. Take the meat off the bones, if you wish.

Return the meat and cranberries to the casserole, season carefully with salt and pepper, and serve the ribs over a low bed of tender gnocchi.

Yield: 4 servings

Tipsy Latina Thighs

This zesty treatment for meaty chicken thighs is kind of a rapid approach to fried chicken, with three times the flavor. You can step up the heat by adding more chipotle peppers and/or Tabasco sauce to the marinade—and by marinating overnight. You can heighten the flavor by toasting and grinding your own spices. And if you want Latino thighs, find yourself a quartet of capons.

The Marinade

- 3 cloves garlic, pressed
- 1 teaspoon ground cumin
- ½ teaspoon ground mace
- 1 teaspoon sweet paprika
- 1 teaspoon ground coriander seeds
- 2 packed tablespoons fresh cilantro leaves
- Several grinds of black pepper
- 2 teaspoons soy sauce
- Juice of 1 orange
- Juice of 1 lime
- ¼ cup pineapple juice
- ¼ cup apple cider
- ¼ cup tequila
- 1 tablespoon olive oil
- 2 (or more) chipotle peppers, canned in adobo sauce
- A few teaspoons of that adobo sauce
- Droplets of Tabasco sauce to taste

8 meaty chicken thighs, about three pounds, skin on and bone in
Canola oil, for frying at ¼-inch depth
1 cup all-purpose flour

1 teaspoon salt
1 teaspoon freshly ground black pepper
1 teaspoon dried thyme
½ cup dry, unseasoned bread crumbs

In a cylindrical container about 1 inch wider in circumference than the business end of your immersion blender, puree the marinade ingredients. Place the thighs in a sealable plastic bag and pour the marinade over them. Seal the bag and massage the thighs with the marinade. Marinate the ingredients for 1 hour to overnight in the refrigerator, turning the bag at least once.

Preheat the oven to 400°F. Place a cast-iron skillet large enough to hold the thighs in a single layer over medium-high heat. After 7 minutes, carefully pour ¼ inch of canola oil into the skillet.

Meanwhile, season the flour with the salt, pepper, and thyme, then stir in the dried bread crumbs. Mix well.

Dredge the thighs in the flour mixture and fry them in the hot oil for 4 minutes on each side. Transfer the thighs to a foil-lined baking sheet and bake on your oven's highest rack setting for 15 minutes, or until the juices run clear at the thickest part of the largest thigh. Serve the thighs hot or at room temperature (after letting them rest on a rack), with a cooling, creamy coleslaw, buttered mashed potatoes, and a full-bodied, icy Riesling or a well-chilled Mexican beer.

Yield: 4 servings

Lamb Meatballs with
Pimiento–Crème Fraîche Sauce

*This is a fairly busy, but utterly delicious dish, based on a tapa I had
in Barcelona.*

½ cup chopped pimientos, from a jar
2 cups chicken broth
½ cup crème fraîche, plus more for serving
Minced zest of 1 scrubbed lemon
5 saffron threads
1 pound ground lamb
1 large egg, lightly beaten
2 cloves garlic, pressed
2 tablespoons minced cilantro
2 teaspoons minced thyme leaves
1 teaspoon bittersweet smoked Spanish paprika
2 teaspoons kosher salt
2 tablespoons canola oil
½ teaspoon cinnamon
2 tablespoons chopped green olives
1 cup steamed basmati rice
Preserved lemon (optional)

In a 1-quart glass measure, using an immersion blender, puree the
pimientos with the broth, crème fraîche, lemon zest, and saffron
threads. In a microwave oven, bring the mixture just to a simmer.
(Timing varies according to your oven's wattage. Start checking af-

ter 2 minutes on high.) Set the mixture aside to let the flavors commingle.

In a large bowl, combine the lamb, egg, garlic, cilantro, thyme, and paprika. Add the salt. Using your hands, gently mix, then form into eight 2-inch meatballs.

In a large skillet, heat the oil over medium-high heat until it slides easily across the skillet. Add the meatballs and brown them all over, about 8 minutes. Slide the meatballs to one side of the pan. Add the red pepper sauce, the cinnamon, and the green olives. Bring the mixture just to a boil. Simmer the meatballs over moderately low heat, stirring and turning them occasionally in the sauce, until the sauce reduces slightly, 12 minutes. Taste carefully and season with salt, if needed.

Make rice rings on two plates. Divide the meatballs between the plates, spoon plenty of the sauce over the meatballs and the rice, and serve with a dollop or two of crème fraîche and a slice or two of preserved lemon, if desired.

Yield: 2 servings

Tuna Steaks Puttanesca

Rough and rusty, this fairly intense sauce goes famously well with pasta, but this version is really enthralling on tuna. I like my tuna red rare, if not actually raw, but you should sauté the tuna to your liking. This sauce also works well with salmon or even swordfish steaks. Be sure to pit your own Kalamata olives. Pre-pitted olives are soggy.

4 tablespoons extra virgin olive oil
4 cloves garlic, pressed into a glass measure, covered with 1
    tablespoon water
Droplets of Tabasco sauce to taste
8 anchovy fillets, rinsed well and finely chopped
1 tablespoon fresh marjoram or oregano leaves
2 teaspoons finely grated lemon zest
2 teaspoons balsamic vinegar
¼ cup dry white vermouth
½ cup fish or chicken stock
1 medium ripe tomato, skinned and diced, or 1 cup canned
    diced tomato
1 tablespoon tomato paste
¾ cup Kalamata olives, pitted and coarsely chopped
2 tablespoons capers, rinsed
4 thick tuna steaks

In a saucepan, heat 2 tablespoons of the olive oil over medium heat until it rolls quickly across the pan. Add the garlic/water mixture, Tabasco to taste, and the chopped anchovies. Stir for 3 minutes. Add the marjoram, lemon zest, balsamic vinegar, ver-

mouth, and stock. Add the tomato, tomato paste, olives, and capers and simmer the sauce over medium-low heat for 10 minutes, with a splatter screen in place. Turn off the heat, puree the sauce roughly with an immersion blender, pulsing just until a rough-and-tumble sauce is created. You may want to thicken the sauce by simmering it for 10 to 20 minutes.

In a skillet large enough to hold the tuna steaks in a single layer, heat the remaining 2 tablespoons of olive oil over medium-high heat. Sear the tuna on each side for 1 minute. Continue cooking and turning the tuna (or not) until it reaches your desired level of doneness.

Serve the tuna steaks dribbled generously with the sauce.

Yield: 4 servings

Grilled Lime Chicken with Fontina Cheese and Dried Chile Puree

If you can't get fresh oregano, use 1 tablespoon of chopped fresh thyme leaves. The chicken needs to marinate overnight, so plan accordingly.

⅓ cup fresh lime juice, from about 3 heavy limes
2 cloves garlic
2 teaspoons freshly grated ginger
¼ cup dry white vermouth
4 tablespoons soy sauce
3 tablespoons canola oil, plus additional for brushing grill
1 tablespoon light brown sugar
1 teaspoon turmeric
½ teaspoon ground cinnamon
½ teaspoon ground mace
1 tablespoon chopped fresh oregano leaves
2 heaping teaspoons chopped fresh rosemary leaves
2 canned chipotle chiles, with 1 tablespoon of the adobo they're canned with
4 skinless, boneless chicken breast halves
1 cup grated Fontina cheese
¼ cup chopped scallions
Dried Chile Sauce (recipe follows)
¼ cup chopped scallions

Squeeze the lime juice into a 1-cup glass measure. Press the garlic into a 1-quart glass measure and quickly add the lime juice. Whisk in the ginger, vermouth, soy sauce, oil, sugar, turmeric, cinnamon, mace, oregano, rosemary, and chipotle chiles. Puree the marinade with an immersion blender, tilting the glass measure if necessary.

Place the chicken in a sealable plastic bag and pour the marinade over. Press the air out of the bag and massage the marinade into the chicken for a few minutes. Refrigerate the chicken overnight, turning the bag occasionally.

Bring a charcoal fire to high heat. Carefully brush the grate lightly with canola oil. Remove the chicken breasts from the marinade, discarding the marinade, and grill the chicken until just cooked through, turning occasionally, about 8 minutes. Quickly divide the Fontina cheese among the breasts, cover the grill or tent the chicken with foil, and grill until the cheese melts, about 1½ minutes more. Plate the chicken and serve dribbled generously with Dried Chile Sauce, and scattered with the scallions. Pass extra sauce at the table. It goes nicely on crusty bread.

Yield: 4 servings

Dried Chile Sauce

Ancho chiles can be mild or very spicy; dried chipotles are pretty hot. Proceed according to your capsaicin needs.

2 dried ancho chiles, stemmed, seeded, and torn into pieces
1 dried New Mexican chile, stemmed, seeded, and torn into pieces
2 dried chipotle chiles (or more if you want more heat), stemmed, seeded, and torn into pieces
2 cups chicken stock, low sodium if canned
2 tablespoons fresh lime juice
½ cup crème fraîche
2 tablespoons dark brown sugar
1 tablespoon chopped fresh oregano
1 teaspoon chopped fresh rosemary
½ teaspoon ground cumin
½ teaspoon ground coriander
1 teaspoon Chinese five-spice powder
Salt and freshly ground black pepper

Place the chiles in a 1-quart glass measure, cover them with the chicken stock, and bring the mixture to a boil in a microwave oven. (Time will vary according to the microwave oven's wattage.) Let the chiles stand until they're very soft, about 40 minutes. Drain them, filtering and reserving ½ cup of the soaking liquid.

With an immersion blender, puree the chiles in the glass measure with ¼ cup of the soaking liquid and the lime juice. Add the crème fraîche, brown sugar, oregano, rosemary, cumin, coriander, and five-spice powder. Puree the mixture with the immersion blender until smooth. Season to taste with salt and pepper. Add a little more of the soaking liquid if the sauce needs thinning, but more likely you'll want to thicken the sauce by simmering it for 10 to 20 minutes. Refrigerate, covered, until ready to use, then microwave the sauce, stirring thoroughly every 30 seconds, until hot.

Yield: 1½ cups

Chicken in Pimiento Cream Sauce

Serve this with basmati rice all showered with freshly chopped parsley.

1 teaspoon cumin seeds
1 teaspoon caraway seeds
4 meaty chicken drumsticks and 6 thighs
Salt and freshly ground black pepper
1 tablespoon sweet smoked Spanish paprika
All-purpose flour, for dusting
2 tablespoons canola oil
½ cup dry white vermouth
1 medium onion, thinly sliced
2 large cloves garlic, pressed
2 tablespoons unsalted butter
One 14-ounce can diced tomatoes in juice (preferably Muir Glen)
1 teaspoon minced thyme leaves
2 tablespoons minced marjoram leaves (or oregano leaves, or
    more thyme)
1 scant tablespoon ketchup
1 bay leaf
1 cup chicken broth
¼ cup crème fraîche, or more to taste
One 2-ounce bottle pimientos, drained and sliced into ¼-inch strips
½ cup pitted green Spanish or Provençal olives, roughly
    chopped
2 cups cooked basmati rice
1 tablespoon minced parsley

Toast the cumin and caraway seeds over moderate heat for about
a minute or until fragrant. In a spice grinder, grind the seeds to a
fine powder.

Season the chicken with salt and pepper and dust with half the paprika. Lightly dust with flour. Heat the oil in a large enameled cast-iron casserole. Add the chicken, skin side down, in batches and fry over moderately high heat until the skin is well browned. Transfer the chicken to a plate.

Deglaze the casserole with ¼ cup of the vermouth. Lower the heat to moderate and add the onion, garlic, and butter to the casserole and cook over moderate heat, stirring, until the onion softens, about 5 minutes. Add the ground cumin and caraway and the rest of the paprika (about 2 teaspoons) and cook, stirring, until fragrant, about 2 minutes.

Stir in the diced tomatoes, thyme, marjoram, ketchup, and bay leaf, and cook, stirring, for 1 minute. Stir in the remaining ¼ cup of vermouth and simmer for 1 minute. Add the broth, season with salt and pepper, and bring to a simmer.

Return the chicken to the casserole along with any accumulated juices. Cover and simmer over low heat for 20 to 25 minutes, until the chicken is cooked through. Transfer the chicken to a clean plate.

Add the crème fraîche to the sauce and simmer for 5 minutes. Discard the bay leaf. Stir in half of the pimiento strips. With an immersion blender, puree the sauce well. Stir in a few more tablespoons of crème fraîche—why not?—return the chicken to the sauce, stir in the olives, and bring to a simmer.

Serve the chicken with a small pile of rice dribbled with the sauce, garnished with the remaining pimiento strips, and sprinkled with the parsley.

Yield: 3 to 4 servings

Mexican Casserole: Chilaquiles

Salsa Verde
    16 small tomatillos, husks removed and rinsed
    1½ cups chicken broth
    1 poblano chile
    1 small onion, quartered
    3 cloves garlic, chopped
    1 cup loosely packed fresh cilantro leaves
    1 tablespoon peanut oil
    Salt and pepper

Fried Tortillas
    8 to 10 corn tortillas
    1 cup canola oil

    2 to 3 Mexican-style (soft, uncooked) chorizos (D'Artagnan
        preferred), thinly sliced, or shredded roasted chicken, tossed
        with a little of your favorite chili powder
    8 ounces mozzarella cheese, sliced
    8 ounces queso fresco or Asiago fresco, crumbled (1½ cups)
    Crème fraîche or sour cream, for garnish
    1 ripe avocado, halved, pitted, carved into cubes right in the
        husk, and spooned out

Make the salsa: Place the tomatillos in a medium saucepan.
Cover with the chicken broth and bring to a boil. Reduce the
heat and simmer for 10 minutes, or until the tomatillos begin to
soften. Remove from the heat and set aside to cool.
    Roast the poblano pepper over an open flame or under a hot

broiler, turning to blacken the skin on all sides. Steam the pepper in a plastic bag for 15 minutes. Remove it and rub off the blackened skin with a paper towel. Do not rinse! Discard the seeds and stem and roughly chop the poblano flesh.

When the tomatillo mixture has cooled, add the poblano, onion, garlic, and cilantro to the saucepan and blend with an immersion blender for 3 minutes until everything is pureed and smooth.

Heat a roomy skillet over medium heat and add the peanut oil. When the oil is hot, add the puree. Cook, stirring often to prevent sticking, for 10 minutes, to thicken the sauce. Taste carefully and season with salt and pepper. Remove the skillet from the heat and set it aside.

Fry the tortillas: Stack the tortillas and quarter them with a knife. Heat the canola oil in a large skillet over medium-high heat until hot but not smoking, about 350°F on a deep-frying thermometer. Fry the tortillas in batches, without crowding the pan, for about 2 minutes, or until golden brown and crispy. Remove with a skimmer to paper towels to drain. Salt to taste.

Preheat the oven to 350°F. Lightly oil a 10- to 12-inch enameled cast-iron oval gratin or other suitable casserole dish. Place a layer of fried tortilla pieces in the bottom of the dish and cover with a layer of chicken or chorizo and each of the two cheeses. Spoon some of the salsa over the cheese. Repeat the layers until all the ingredients are used, finishing with the salsa. Cover the dish with foil.

Bake the casserole for 30 to 40 minutes, until bubbly all over and golden brown on top.

Serve the casserole topped with a dollop of crème fraîche or sour cream and a scattering of avocado cubes.

Yield: 3 servings

Pastel de Choclo:
Chilean Shepherd's Pie

This is a vibrant variation on a classic Chilean casserole that blends beef, chicken, and shrimp—each with a distinct flavor—under a very creamy blanket of sweet corn. Here I use ground buffalo and chunks of boneless rabbit, both available from www.dartagnan .com. It's fun to fuss over the ingredients, and to make your own variation using whatever you have on hand. The dish comes together very quickly if you have everything chopped and at the ready and the oven preheated before you turn on the stovetop: mise en place.

And if you happen to have leftover corn on the cob and a couple of grilled steaks, Pastel de choclo *is your very best bet.*

For the casserole:
  3 medium yellow onions, peeled and finely chopped
  3 tablespoons extra virgin olive oil
  2 pounds ground buffalo (*or* leftover grilled steak, cut into bite-
      sized chunks, which you would merely reheat; see below)
  1½ pounds boneless rabbit, cut into bite-sized chunks
  2 teaspoons lemon zest, finely minced
  2 tablespoons all-purpose flour
  2 teaspoons kosher salt
  Dashes of Tabasco sauce
  ⅓ cup low-salt beef broth
  ¾ cup sliced green olives stuffed with pimientos

3 to 4 hot chile peppers, such as jalapeño (hot), Serrano (hotter), and/or habanero (hottest)

¼ cup golden raisins, soaked for 15 minutes in warmed Madeira wine or sweet vermouth to cover, then drained

2 tablespoons capers, packed in salt and very thoroughly rinsed, chopped if large

½ teaspoon ground cumin

1 teaspoon toasted sesame seeds

½ teaspoon toasted caraway seeds

¾ pound rock shrimp, or medium shrimp, shelled, cleaned, and deveined (optional, but you'll miss them if you skip them)

For the Topping

(1 of the chopped onions reserved from above)

3 tablespoons unsalted butter

2 cups grated fresh corn (about 4 ears), cobs scraped with the dull side of a knife, *or* 2 cups frozen kernels combined with ½ to 1 cup canned "creamed" corn

6 large egg yolks

½ cup heavy cream

½ teaspoon cinnamon

¼ teaspoon allspice

¼ teaspoon mace

2 teaspoons sugar

3 hard-cooked eggs, quartered (optional)

3 tablespoons melted unsalted butter, for brushing the optional eggs

Preheat the oven to 350°F. In a very large sauté pan over moderate heat, sauté two-thirds of the chopped onions in the oil for 6 to 7 minutes, until soft and beginning to color. Add the ground buffalo and sauté just until the pinkness begins to disappear. (If using grilled sirloin chunks, just heat them through and proceed with the rabbit.) Add the rabbit and sauté for 4 to 5 minutes, until it is just cooked through. Stir in the lemon zest and sprinkle with flour, salt, and Tabasco sauce, stirring for just a few minutes. Pour in the broth and cook over low heat for 5 minutes, stirring slowly. Add the olives, chiles, raisins, capers, cumin, and sesame and caraway seeds. Stir in the shrimp and cook just 2 minutes longer. If the mixture seems too soupy, drain a bit of the liquid out.

Immediately turn the mixture into a buttered baking pan large enough to fill by at least 1½ inches (12 × 10½ × 2½ inches should do nicely). Cover the pan and keep warm.

To make the topping: In the same large skillet, over moderate heat, sauté the remaining chopped onion in the butter until softened, 5 minutes. Mix in the corn and 1 teaspoon salt and cook for 2 minutes over low heat, stirring. In a medium mixing bowl, with an immersion blender, beat together the egg yolks, cream, spices, and sugar. Turn off the heat and stir the egg mixture into the corn mixture. Pulse the immersion blender in the mixture until it's roughly pureed—not completely smooth! Spread the corn mixture evenly over the meat. Decorate the topping with the quartered hard-cooked eggs, if using, and brush them lightly with the melted butter. Bake, uncovered, for 20 minutes or until bubbly.

Just before serving, you might want to provide the dish with a caramelized topping—*pastel de choclo brûlée*. Scatter a few table-spoons of brown sugar evenly over the top and run the dish under a hot broiler until the sugar melts and bubbles.

Yield: 6 to 8 servings

Grilled Spicy Pork Tenderloin with Honey Mustard Sauce

The deeply flavored, spicy marinade in this recipe makes enough to double the pork, or it may be used with chicken breasts or thighs, lamb chops, or flank steak. The bean-chili sauce I call for is usually available in many Asian markets, at Whole Foods, and here: http://www.vnsupermarket.com/beansauces.php. Substitute at your own risk—some Chinese bean-chili sauces are way too salty, and others are so hot your ears will emit steam. As it is, this is spicy enough to sting your eyes from the smoke that rises as it grills. So watch it! I once sent my friends sobbing into the street when I grilled these on an indoor grill. For maximum flavor, marinate the meat overnight.

2 whole pork tenderloins, about 2 pounds

For the Marinade
    3 tablespoons sesame seeds
    1 cup hoisin sauce
    1 tablespoon sugar
    1 tablespoon sesame oil
    2 tablespoons soy sauce
    2 tablespoons dry sherry
    2 tablespoons sherry-wine vinegar
    2 tablespoons mirin (rice-wine vinegar)
    2 scallions, white and light green parts only, minced
    3 tablespoons Lan Chi Bean Sauce with Chili
    2 teaspoons freshly grated ginger
    2 tablespoons minced garlic

½ teaspoon freshly ground black pepper
Hot Honey Mustard (recipe follows)

Trim any silver skin from the tenderloins and place them in a sealable plastic bag.

Toast the sesame seeds in a covered, small, dry skillet over medium-low heat until the seeds are golden, fragrant, and popping, about 3 minutes. Let them cool, then pulverize them lightly in a spice grinder or using a mortar and pestle. (Don't overdo it in the spice grinder, or you'll have sesame butter.)

Combine the crushed seeds with the remaining ingredients in a medium bowl. Puree the mixture well with an immersion blender. Pour about half the marinade over the tenderloins, press out any air in the bag, seal it, and refrigerate for 3 hours, or overnight, if possible. Reserve the remaining marinade for another use (see headnote).

Heat a grill pan over medium-high heat, or bring an electric grill to high heat, and open the windows. Or, better, prepare a hot fire in an outdoor grill. Remove the tenderloins from the marinade, and place on a grill pan or electric grill. Sear the meat on both sides (4 inches from the coals, if you're outdoors), turning after 2½ minutes. Lower the heat (or move the tenderloins to a cooler part of the grill) and grill, turning occasionally, until the tenderloin reaches an internal temperature of 140 to 145°F for medium rare. Remove the tenderloins from the heat and tent with foil. Let the meat rest for 5 minutes before slicing into medallions.

Serve the tenderloins as is or gild the lily by drizzling the medalions with Hot Honey Mustard (see recipe on
p. 124).

Yield: 4 servings

Hot Honey Mustard

This, too, makes too much for one recipe. But it keeps well, chilled, for a few weeks, and the mustard really beautifies a rare roast beef sandwich. You could do this in a regular 1-quart saucepan if you're careful to prevent the eggs from curdling—placing it on and off medium heat as it nears a boil and stirring constantly.

2 large eggs
⅔ cup dry mustard, Coleman's preferred
½ cup honey
⅔ cup distilled white vinegar
¼ teaspoon vanilla extract

Place all the ingredients in the top of a double boiler. Blend well with an immersion blender. Cook the mixture over simmering water, stirring occasionally, until the mixture is thick enough to form ribbons when it's drizzled from a spoon, 10 to 15 minutes. Remove the mixture from the heat and allow the mustard to cool. Refrigerate it in an airtight container to chill and thicken further.

Yield: about 2 cups

Nice Messy
Summer Sandwiches for Two

These are addictively delicious and easy to double or even triple if you're entertaining a crowd. And you won't have to heat up your kitchen—the warm sandwich is assembled using only a microwave oven. You may have to adjust the melting time, depending on the wattage of your microwave oven.

1 large ripe tomato
½ teaspoon salt
6 slices good bacon
2 fresh, soft, 8-inch "hero"-style rolls (Portuguese rolls)
Mayonnaise
¼ cup crumbled Stilton cheese
Fresh thyme leaves
Freshly ground black pepper

Peel, seed, juice, and coarsely chop the tomato. Place it in an immersion blender–friendly cup or cylindrical container and pulse the tomato with the blender until it's finely chopped. Transfer the tomato to cheesecloth or a fine sieve set over a bowl, stir in the salt, and let it drain for ½ hour, pressing down on the tomato 2 to 3 times.

Meanwhile, place the bacon on layers of microwavable paper towels and microwave the bacon until it's done to your liking.

(Timing will vary, depending on the wattage of your oven.) Let the bacon drain on paper towels.

Split the hero rolls and slather them with mayonnaise. Dot the mayonnaise with crumbled Stilton cheese to taste.

When the chopped tomato has drained, divide it between the 2 sandwiches on 2 plates.

Lay the tomato across the cheese, and sprinkle lightly with the thyme leaves and pepper. Tear the bacon slices in half, and lay them across the tomato. Microwave the sandwich, opened and uncovered, for 20 to 30 seconds on high or until it is slightly melted. Fold into a sandwich and serve at once on large plates with iced tea and plenty of napkins.

You can use turkey bacon, and some of the "infused" commercial mayonnaises are wonderful. Thin slices of red onion might also be welcome. But something about the pure Stilton/bacon/tomato combo puts quite a bounce in your summer step.

Yield: 2 sandwiches

SIDE DISHES

Asparagus with Mayonnaise Verte

Soaking peeled stalks of thick asparagus in lightly sugared water be-
fore roasting them in a very hot oven helps to caramelize them. Serve
this as an appetizer at room temperature, or warm as a side dish.

1½ pounds thick asparagus, dry ends snapped off and stalks
　　peeled
2 to 3 tablespoons sugar
5 tablespoons olive oil
Sea salt and freshly ground black pepper
½ cup packed Italian parsley leaves (no stems)
1 tablespoon lime juice
1 teaspoon smooth Dijon mustard, Maille preferred
½ cup mayonnaise
¼ cup mascarpone, crème fraîche, or sour cream
1 pinch dried tarragon
½ teaspoon orange zest, from a scrubbed or organic orange
Spanish (smoked) paprika, for sprinkling the mayonnaise
　　(optional)

Soak the peeled asparagus for an hour or two in a few quarts of
cool water with 2 to 3 tablespoons of sugar dissolved in it. Keep
refrigerated.

　Preheat the oven to 425°F. Arrange the asparagus in one layer
on a foil-lined jelly-roll pan. Drizzle with 3 tablespoons of the
olive oil and roll the spears to coat them. Sprinkle judiciously
with salt and pepper. Roast the asparagus for 15 to 20 minutes,
until just tender.

Choose a cylindrical container wide enough to accommodate an immersion blender with about an extra inch of diameter. Place the parsley, the remaining 2 tablespoons olive oil, the lime juice, mustard, mayonnaise, mascarpone, tarragon, and orange zest in the container. Puree the ingredients with an immersion blender, scraping down the sides of the container with a rubber spatula several times. Taste for salt and pepper. Stir the mixture well.

Serve the asparagus hot, warm, or at room temperature. Place the mayonnaise mixture in individual dipping ramekins or in one large ramekin, sprinkled with the paprika, if desired.

Yield: 3 to 4 side dish servings, 5 to 6 appetizer portions

Cauliflower Soufflé

Here is another slightly retro recipe, but everything old is new again these days. A nice fluffy way to ingest your cruciferous vegetables!

1 medium head cauliflower, about 1½ pounds, cut into florets
5 tablespoons unsalted butter, softened
½ cup Panko crumbs, or dry bread crumbs
⅓ cup grated Parmigiano-Reggiano cheese
½ cup milk
1 teaspoon kosher salt
4 large eggs, separated
½ teaspoon freshly ground white pepper
¼ cup flour
¼ to ½ cup crumbled Stilton cheese (optional)
¼ teaspoon cream of tartar

Place the cauliflower florets in a steamer basket over an inch of boiling water. Cover the steamer and cook the cauliflower for 8 to 9 minutes, or until tender. Let the cauliflower cool.

Prepare a 2-quart soufflé dish: Grease the inside of the soufflé dish with 1 tablespoon of the butter. Scatter the crumbs and grated Parmigiano-Reggiano all over the inside of the buttered dish.

Preheat the oven to 350°F. Break the cooked cauliflower into florets and place them in a large bowl. Pour the milk over the florets and puree the mixture with an immersion blender, pulsing until smooth. Add the salt, egg yolks, white pepper, flour, and the remaining 4 tablespoons butter. Puree the mixture again until very smooth. Stir in the crumbled Stilton, if using, to taste.

Beat the egg whites with the cream of tartar, using an electric standing mixer or handheld electric mixer, until stiff peaks form. Fold one-quarter of the stiff egg whites into the cauliflower mixture, folding until fully incorporated. Fold the rest of the egg whites into the mixture. Turn into the prepared soufflé dish and bake for 40 to 45 minutes. Serve the soufflé promptly.

Yield: 4 to 6 servings

Frijoles

I like fairly spicy food, as you may have noticed by now. If you don't, hold back on the chiles—or seed them if you're in between. Contrary to popular belief, though, the seeds pick up their heat from the white inner ribs of these chiles, where the real punch lies.

1 pound dry pinto beans
2 tablespoons unhydrogenated lard, preferably rendered leaf lard
¼ pound pancetta, finely chopped
1½ cups chopped white onions
1 serrano chile, stemmed and finely chopped, or more to taste
1 jalapeño chile, stemmed and finely chopped, or more to taste
6 cloves garlic
1 teaspoon cumin seeds, toasted and finely ground
1 teaspoon dried oregano, preferably Mexican
Salt to taste

In the large pot you will later use to cook them, soak the beans in cold water to cover by 4 inches overnight. Drain and rinse well.

Heat 1 tablespoon of the lard in a stockpot over medium heat. Add the pancetta and cook for 4 minutes, then add 1 cup of the onions and the chopped chiles and sauté for 5 minutes. Press 2 of the garlic cloves with a sturdy garlic press into the onions and stir well for 1 minute.

Add the drained beans, 6 cups of filtered water, cumin, and oregano. Raise the heat to high, bring to a boil, reduce the heat to low, cover, and simmer for 45 minutes.

Add a judicious amount of salt, stir well, and continue to simmer for 30 to 35 minutes, or until the beans are quite tender. You'll have about 7 cups of beans.

In a large deep skillet, heat the remaining tablespoon of lard over medium heat. Add the remaining ½ cup of onion and cook until browned, about 5 minutes. Press the remaining 4 cloves of garlic into the onions and stir well for 1 minute. Add 3½ cups of the cooked beans and 1 cup of their cooking liquid to the skillet. Puree the mixture with an immersion blender until creamy and smooth, adding more liquid or beans if necessary. Season the frijoles to taste with salt and serve warm.

Yield: 6 servings

Fresh Corn Pudding

This is a variation on a childhood favorite. Unfortunately, this dish can be made only in high summer with the freshest possible local corn.

4 to 5 ears corn
1½ cups soft white bread crumbs
Canola oil, for greasing the baking dish
1 tablespoon minced red bell pepper
2 medium shallots, minced
1 cup half-and-half, or whole milk if you want a lighter pudding
2 large eggs
Salt and freshly ground black pepper to taste
2 to 3 scallions, white and light green parts only, minced

Preheat the oven to 375°F. Over a large bowl, cut the kernels from the corncobs with a sharp paring knife, then scrape the cobs with the back of the knife to get all the "milk" you can into the corn.

Pour the crumbs into a lightly oiled 1½-quart gratin or baking dish. Sprinkle the minced red pepper over the crumbs. Place the shallots, half-and-half, eggs, corn, and salt and pepper in a 1-quart glass measure. Puree the mixture for 30 seconds with an immersion blender. Slowly pour the mixture over the crumbs and red pepper. Stir lightly, then bake until a skewer comes out clean when inserted in the center of the pudding, about 1 hour. Serve the pudding at once, scattered with the minced scallions.

Yield: 4 servings

PASTA

Fusilli with Roasted Asparagus, Pancetta, Red Bell Pepper, and Peppercorn Goat Cheese Sauce

This is one of my favorite pasta recipes. I came up with it when I went into a kind of trance at my farmer's market because the Coach Farms farmer put a melting slab of green peppercorn goat's milk cheese in my mouth.

2 to 3 tablespoons sugar
1 pound medium asparagus, dry ends snapped off and any thicker stalks peeled
3 tablespoons extra virgin olive oil
Sea salt and freshly ground black pepper
1 meaty red bell pepper
½ pound pancetta, chopped if it's thinly sliced, sliced into ¼-inch pieces if it's in a slab
2 tablespoons dry white vermouth or water
1½ cups heavy cream, or crème fraîche
6 ounces firm green peppercorn goat cheese, aged 1 to 2 months, including rind, if any, or 6 ounces firm goat cheese and 1 tablespoon brined green peppercorns, drained and rinsed
1 pound dried fusilli

Dissolve the sugar in a quart of cool water and soak the asparagus for an hour or two.

Start bringing a large pot of salted water to a boil. Preheat the oven to 425°F. Arrange the asparagus in one layer on a foil-lined jelly-roll pan. Drizzle with 2 tablespoons of the olive oil and roll the spears to coat them. Season lightly with the sea salt and pepper. Roast the asparagus for 12 minutes. Let them cool. Slice the asparagus crosswise into 1½-inch pieces and set them aside.

Meanwhile, stem and seed the pepper, cut it along its vertical ridges into 3 to 4 pieces, and with a swiveling vegetable peeler, peel the skin of each piece with a gentle sawing motion. Slice the pepper into ½-inch strips, about 1½ inches long.

Pour the remaining tablespoon of olive oil into a large stainless sauté pan about 2 inches deep and set it over medium heat. When the oil rolls easily across the pan's surface, add the pancetta and sauté for 4 to 5 minutes, stirring every minute or so. Deglaze the skillet with the vermouth and add the pepper strips. Lower the heat, and let the mixture simmer for 5 minutes, stirring every so often.

Meanwhile, pour the cream into a small (1-quart) saucepan and bring to a boil over medium-high heat. Slice the goat cheese into ½-inch cubes. Just when the cream begins to scald, lower the heat and toss in the cheese cubes. After 1 minute, blend the mixture with an immersion blender. Season lightly with salt and pepper and keep warm.

Boil the fusilli until it is al dente, according to the manufacturer's instructions, about 12 minutes. Drain it well. In a large serving bowl (or right in the sauté pan), toss the fusilli with the pepper, pancetta, and asparagus pieces. With the immersion blender, buzz the hot cream sauce until it's foamy, then pour it over the pasta mixture and toss well. Serve hot.

Yield: 4 servings

Fettuccine Alfredo with
Roasted Red Pepper

This rich and pretty pink sauce has plenty of oomph. If you can find bottled Spanish piquillo peppers, by all means substitute them for the roasted red bell pepper.

1 large red bell pepper (see headnote)
8 tablespoons unsalted butter
2 cloves garlic
2 cups heavy cream
1½ cups freshly grated Parmigiano-Reggiano cheese
2 teaspoons freshly ground white pepper
½ teaspoon freshly grated nutmeg
1 pound fresh fettuccine
Roughly chopped toasted walnuts (optional)

Roast the red pepper over a gas flame or under a hot broiler, turning frequently, until blackened all over. Transfer the pepper to a plastic bag and let the pepper steam for 15 minutes. With paper towels, rub the blackened skin off the pepper. Do not rinse. Stem and seed the pepper, chop it roughly, and set aside.

Meanwhile, bring a large pot of salted water to a boil. In a medium saucepan, melt the butter over medium heat. Press the garlic cloves into the butter through a sturdy garlic press. Raise the heat to medium-high, add the cream, and bring nearly to a boil, stirring often. Lower the heat and let the sauce simmer for 5 minutes, still stirring often. Add the cheese, ¼ cup at a time, stirring constantly until it melts after each addition. Stir in the white pepper and nutmeg.

Add the chopped pepper to the sauce and puree well with an immersion blender.

Cook the fettuccine according to the manufacturer's instructions. Drain it well, and toss with the sauce until every strand is coated. Serve the fettuccine at once, with a scattering of chopped toasted walnuts, if desired.

Yield: 4 servings

Roasted Spaghetti

Taking comfort food right to the limit, this delightfully decadent Friday night special will bring out all sorts of inner children.

2 tablespoons olive oil
1 large yellow onion, minced
2 cloves garlic, minced
1 pound ground chuck
½ pound sweet Italian sausage, casings removed, meat crumbled
Salt and freshly ground black pepper
1 teaspoon dried oregano
1 teaspoon dried thyme
⅓ cup milk
¼ cup dry vermouth
1 recipe Tomato-Cream Pasta Sauce (recipe follows)
2 tablespoons finely chopped flat-leaf parsley
⅔ cup crème fraîche
1 pound spaghetti, broken in half
½ pound sharp Cheddar cheese, grated (about 2 cups)

Preheat the oven to 375°F. In a large cast-iron skillet (at least 12 inches in diameter and 2½ inches deep) or a large enameled cast-iron Dutch oven, heat the olive oil and sauté the onion and garlic over medium heat until lightly browned, about 8 minutes.

Add the ground chuck and sausage, sprinkle the meat with a generous amount of salt and pepper, and brown, breaking up the chunks with a wooden spoon. Sprinkle in the oregano and thyme, then stir in the milk. Let the mixture bubble for 10 minutes, then stir in the vermouth and simmer for 5 minutes before adding the tomato-cream pasta sauce, parsley, and crème fraîche.

Meanwhile, cook the halved spaghetti in a large pot of boiling well-salted water, just until al dente, 9 minutes *tops*. Just before draining, add ½ cup of the cooking water to the sauce.

Drain the pasta well and stir it into the simmering sauce with half the grated cheese. Cover with the remaining cheese and transfer the skillet to the preheated oven. Bake for 30 minutes, or until the spaghetti strands poking up through the cheese are nice and crispy.

Yield: 4 ample servings

Tomato-Cream Pasta Sauce

*This makes a perfect dressing for freshly made gnocchi, spaghetti,
rigatoni, or penne, or use it here in the Roasted Spaghetti.*

2 tablespoons unsalted butter
1 tablespoon olive oil
1 medium onion, diced
1 clove garlic, pressed
One 14.5-ounce can diced tomatoes, undrained (preferably Muir
    Glen fire-roasted)
2 anchovy fillets, rinsed and minced
2 tablespoons chopped bottled pimiento
1 teaspoon brown sugar
1 teaspoon fresh oregano leaves, or ½ teaspoon dried oregano
Salt and freshly ground black pepper to taste
1 cup heavy cream

In a deep skillet or saucepan over medium heat, melt the butter
in the olive oil. Add the onion and garlic and sauté slowly for 10
minutes, stirring often. Add the tomatoes, anchovies, pimiento,
brown sugar, oregano, and salt and pepper. Bring to a simmer and
let it bubble away for 25 minutes. Turn off the heat, carefully and
thoroughly puree the mixture with an immersion blender. Stir in
the cream, bring the mixture back to a simmer, and cook for another 10 minutes to thicken the sauce, stirring often.

Yield: enough sauce for 1 pound of pasta

Fettuccine with Cantaloupe Sauce

I realize that this sounds *perfectly atrocious, and it is extremely rich, but if I served it to you without telling you the ingredients, you'd lick your plate. As a matter of fact, this recipe is a variation of one that can be traced back to Venice in the 1970s.*

This dish works well in early to mid-September, to signal the end of summer, when cantaloupes are dead ripe. Use fresh pasta to optimize the dish's comforting mouth-feel. You might prefer to use capellini or angel hair pasta. The prosciutto makes this a more grown-up dish, invoking the ubiquitous pairing of prosciutto and melon.

8 tablespoons unsalted butter (1 stick)
1 medium dead-ripe cantaloupe, peeled, seeded, and chopped
    into 1½-inch chunks
¼ cup ketchup
1 cup heavy cream
1 pound fettuccine, fresh preferred, but dried is fine, too
¼ pound thinly sliced prosciutto

Bring a large pot of salted water to a rolling boil. In a large saucepan, melt the butter over medium-low heat. Add the cantaloupe flesh, and gently cook it down, stirring and pressing the cantaloupe with a wooden spoon, for 15 minutes.

Stir in the ketchup and cream. Puree the mixture with an immersion blender until very smooth. Raise the heat to medium, and thicken the sauce for 4 to 5 minutes while you boil the pasta for the appropriate time.

Drain the pasta well and toss it with the hot sauce. Serve it draped with prosciutto, or chop the prosciutto into bite-sized pieces and scatter it over the pasta.

Yield: 3 to 4 servings

DESSERTS

Rhubarb Sorbet

Serve this tangy sorbet plain or over freshly sliced purple plums with a dollop of sour cream and a light sprinkling of brown sugar. Or you could top it with trusty sliced strawberries, a drizzle of balsamic reduction, and a chiffonade of basil—very pretty.

¾ cup sugar
¼ cup brown sugar
1 cup water
3 tablespoons lemon juice
Zest of 1 orange
1 teaspoon vanilla extract
1 pound fresh rhubarb, sliced crosswise into 1-inch pieces, 5 to 6
    stalks
1 teaspoon cognac

In a heavy 2-quart stainless saucepan, combine the sugars, water, lemon juice, zest, and vanilla. Stir over medium-low heat until the sugars dissolve, then raise the heat and bring to a boil. Add the rhubarb, lower the heat, and simmer, covered, until the rhubarb is tender, about 10 minutes.

Let the mixture cool slightly, then puree with an immersion blender, tilting the pan if necessary, then stir in the cognac. Refrigerate the mixture until cold, about 2 hours.

Transfer the mixture to an ice cream maker and freeze according to the manufacturer's instructions. Freeze the sorbet for several hours before serving.

Yield: 1 quart

Peach Sorbet

An August recipe if ever there was one!

  1½ pounds very ripe peaches (about 6 medium), peeled and
    pitted
  ½ cup cold filtered water
  1 cup sugar
  2 tablespoons fresh lemon juice
  1 tablespoon peach brandy

In a roomy metal bowl, thoroughly puree the peaches with the water using an immersion blender. Pour the mixture into a 1-quart container. Add the sugar, lemon juice, and peach brandy to the peach puree. Stir or pulse the puree with the immersion blender to mix well. Cover and refrigerate until very cold, at least 2 hours.

  Stir the mixture to blend it again, and pour it into the canister of an ice cream maker. Freeze according to the manufacturer's directions. Return to the 1-quart container and freeze until firm, at least 3 hours.

  Yield: 3½ cups sorbet

Cider-Pear Sorbet

This is a late autumn sorbet—perfect for Halloween, in fact. Serve the sorbet with a praline poked into it.

1 pound Granny Smith apples, peeled, cored, and finely chopped
1 pound ripe Bartlett pears, peeled, cored, and finely chopped
1 cup apple cider
2 tablespoons Calvados or other apple brandy
1 teaspoon almond extract
½ cup sugar, or more to taste
1 cinnamon stick
4 whole cloves
2 teaspoons roughly grated orange zest
½ cup fresh lemon juice

Combine the apples, pears, ½ cup of the cider, and 1 tablespoon of the Calvados in a medium saucepan over medium heat. Bring to a boil, then reduce the heat to low and simmer, stirring frequently, for 10 minutes, or until the apples and pears have softened. Remove the mixture from the heat, stir in the remaining 1 tablespoon of Calvados and the almond extract, and allow to cool. Puree the mixture thoroughly with an immersion blender. Cover and refrigerate it until thoroughly chilled, at least 1 hour.

In a medium heavy saucepan, combine the sugar with ½ cup of cold filtered water, the cinnamon stick, cloves, and orange zest. Bring the mixture to a boil, stirring, until the sugar is dissolved. Set aside to let the syrup steep for 10 minutes, then add the lemon juice and refrigerate the mixture until thoroughly chilled, at least 1 hour.

Strain the syrup through a fine sieve. Discard the cinnamon stick, cloves, and orange zest. Place 2½ cups of the apple-pear puree in a bowl. Stir in the syrup and the remaining ½ cup of cold cider and blend well with an immersion blender. Pour the mixture into an ice cream machine and freeze according to the manufacturer's instructions.

Yield: about 4 cups

Watermelon Popsicles

Summer on a stick!

1 cup seeded watermelon chunks
1 cup freshly squeezed orange juice
1 cup filtered or bottled water

In a 1-quart glass container, puree the watermelon chunks, orange juice, and water with an immersion blender. Pour the mixture into small wax paper cups on a tray or into a Popsicle mold. Transfer the mixture to the freezer and when it is partially frozen, insert 1 Popsicle stick (or a small plastic spoon) into each Popsicle. When completely frozen, about 4 hours, dip the cups, if used, in hot water to remove the Popsicles.

Yield: enough for 6 servings

Fudgeicles

These are far better than the real thing!

2 cups milk
One 12-ounce can evaporated milk
8 ounces Valrhona or other high-quality bittersweet chocolate,
    melted and cooled
½ cup chocolate Ovaltine, or other powdered chocolate milk mix
2 tablespoons malt powder
1 teaspoon vanilla extract

In a 1-quart glass container, puree the milk, evaporated milk, melted chocolate, Ovaltine, malt powder, and vanilla with an immersion blender. Pour the mixture into small wax paper cups on a tray or into a Popsicle mold. Transfer the mixture to the freezer and when it is partially frozen, insert 1 Popsicle stick (or a small plastic spoon) into each Popsicle. When completely frozen, about 4 hours, dip the cups, if used, in hot water to remove the Popsicles.

Yield: enough for 8 to 10 fudgeicles

Toasted Coconut Ice Cream

Whole lot of chilling going on: Note that the evaporated milk and the coconut milk need to be chilled before you use them. The final mixture requires overnight refrigeration before freezing in an ice cream machine, and at least 3 hours freezing time thereafter, so plan accordingly. Serve with a scattering of macadamia nuts and/or mango or pineapple slices. This ice cream is also remarkably good with heated high-quality chocolate syrup, if that would amuse you.

¾ cup superfine sugar
3 teaspoons cornstarch
½ teaspoon salt
¾ cup milk
1 cup heavy cream
2 large egg yolks
½ cup chilled evaporated milk
1 cup chilled unsweetened canned coconut milk
¼ cup sweetened coconut flakes, *carefully* toasted in a dry pan
  over medium heat

In a medium saucepan, combine the sugar, cornstarch, and salt. Gradually stir in the milk and cream, then blend the mixture with an immersion blender to ream out any lumps. Bring the mixture to a boil, then reduce the heat to a simmer for 1 minute. Remove the pan from the heat.

In a large bowl, beat the egg yolks until well blended, about 30 seconds. Temper the eggs by slowly whisking in ½ cup of the hot milk mixture, then another ½ cup, then pour the mixture into the pan. Heat over medium heat until it reaches 180°F and begins to thicken, stirring *constantly*; it will look like it's about to boil. Remove the pan from the heat and whisk in the chilled evaporated milk and coconut milk, and blend with an immersion blender, again to puree any lumps or bits of egg yolk that might have cooked. The custard may seem slightly thin. Let the mixture cool slightly, then cover tightly with plastic wrap, and refrigerate overnight.

Stir the toasted coconut flakes into the custard and freeze the custard in an ice cream machine according to the manufacturer's instructions, until the ice cream is very thick and cold. Freeze the mixture until it's firm enough to scoop, at least 3 hours.

Yield: about 1 quart

Banana Sherbet

This goes particularly well with chocolate desserts, such as warm brownies.

⅓ cup lemon juice, from 1 to 2 lemons
2 tablespoons light corn syrup
2 teaspoons finely grated lemon zest
⅓ cup sugar
⅛ teaspoon salt
3 medium very ripe bananas, each broken into 4 to 5 pieces
1 very fresh large egg
1 cup milk
1 cup heavy cream
½ cup crème fraîche
1 tablespoon dark rum

Place the lemon juice, corn syrup, and zest in a large bowl. Blend well with the immersion blender. Add the sugar, salt, bananas, and egg. Blend thoroughly with the immersion blender for about 30 seconds.

Combine the mixture with the milk, cream, crème fraîche, and rum and blend once more until thoroughly combined.

Freeze the mixture in an ice cream machine according to the manufacturer's instructions. Freeze the sherbet in your freezer for at least 3 hours before serving.

Yield: 1 quart sherbet

Vanilla–Crème Fraîche Flan

A Cuban favorite, this makes a rich-yet-light finish to any meal. The cream cheese and crème fraîche give the flan a certain oomph.

1 cup sugar, preferably superfine
8 ounces whole milk
One 12-ounce can evaporated milk
One 12-ounce can condensed milk
5 large eggs
4 ounces cream cheese, softened
½ cup crème fraîche
2 teaspoons vanilla extract
1 tablespoon cornstarch

Preheat the oven to 350°F. In a medium saucepan, mix ½ cup of the sugar and a few tablespoons of water, or enough to moisten it. Cook the sugar mixture over low heat until it caramelizes. Carefully swirl the saucepan to coat all sides with the hot caramelized sugar.

In a medium bowl, mix the milks, eggs, cream cheese, crème fraîche, vanilla, cornstarch, and the remaining ½ cup of sugar. With an immersion blender, puree the mixture until it's thoroughly smooth. Pour the mixture into the caramelized sugar saucepan after the sugar has hardened.

Cover the saucepan tightly with foil and place it inside a larger saucepan or other deep oven-proof vessel with enough water in it to come up to 2 inches from the top of the smaller saucepan. Transfer both saucepans to the oven and bake for 90 minutes.

Disassemble the two saucepans. When the flan has cooled for ½ hour or so, uncover it, put a 1-inch-deep platter over the top of the saucepan, and *carefully* invert the saucepan. The flan should come right out. Or simply scoop out servings from the saucepan. Serve the flan warm.

Yield: 6 servings

Peach-Orange Pudding

Other than rice and tapioca, puddings have more or less gone out of favor in the last few decades, and that's a shame, because they have the most comforting texture. This old-fashioned pudding comes together quickly thanks to the immersion blender.

1 envelope unflavored gelatin (2¼ teaspoons)
½ cup hot half-and-half
2 large eggs
½ cup cold milk
3 tablespoons sugar
¼ teaspoon salt
1 cup freshly squeezed orange juice, from 2 to 3 oranges
1 teaspoon finely grated orange zest
1 tablespoon Cointreau, or slightly more to taste
3 medium fresh ripe freestone peaches, peeled, pitted, and cut into 8 pieces
1 cup heavy cream

In the flask that probably came with your immersion blender or a similar container wide enough to accommodate the business end of the blender, buzz the gelatin and the hot half-and-half until they are well combined, 30 seconds or so.

In a large bowl, place the eggs, milk, sugar, salt, orange juice, zest, Cointreau, and peaches. Puree the mixture until smooth, stir in the gelatin mixture, and refrigerate for 45 minutes.

Meanwhile, with the cleaned immersion blender, whip the cream until medium stiff peaks form. Fold the whipped cream into the peach-orange pudding, refrigerate for 30 minutes longer, then spoon the pudding into parfait glasses. Serve the pudding topped with fresh fruit, such as raspberries, blueberries, or more sliced peaches.

Yield: 4 servings

Apple Bread Pudding
with Boozy Custard Sauce

It doesn't get any more comforting than this.

3 tablespoons unsalted butter, softened
6 cups stale 1-inch brioche or other egg bread cubes
6 large eggs
4 cups milk
One 14-ounce can evaporated milk
1 teaspoon freshly grated nutmeg
½ teaspoon ground cinnamon
½ teaspoon ground allspice
¼ teaspoon ground cloves
½ teaspoon salt
1 cup sugar
1 Granny Smith apple
½ cup golden raisins
Boozy Custard Sauce (recipe follows)

Preheat the oven to 350°F. Grease a 13 × 9 × 2-inch baking pan with the butter. Fill the pan nearly to the top with the bread cubes.

In a large bowl, combine the eggs, milk, evaporated milk, nutmeg, cinnamon, allspice, cloves, salt, and sugar. Blend with an immersion blender, until the ingredients are well incorporated.

Core, peel, and dice the apple into ½-inch cubes. Combine the apple with the raisins and spread the mixture over the bread cubes. Toss well with your hands. Pour the milk mixture over the bread and let the mixtures stand for 30 minutes.

Bake the bread pudding, uncovered, for 90 minutes or until jiggly-firm. While the pudding bakes, make the custard sauce that follows. Serve the bread pudding warm dribbled with the custard sauce.

Yield: 12 servings

Boozy Custard Sauce

This sauce was created especially for warm bread pudding.

3 cups milk
1 cup heavy cream
6 large egg yolks
½ cup sugar
½ teaspoon salt
¼ cup good brandy

In a large saucepan, heat the milk and cream slowly over medium-low heat. When the milk is scalded (nearly at a boil), turn off the heat.

Meanwhile, in a medium bowl, whisk the egg yolks until they're pale yellow. Add the sugar and salt.

Slowly add ½ cup of the hot milk, whisking constantly. Add another ½ cup, then add the egg mixture to the rest of the milk in the saucepan. Blend with an immersion blender until well mixed, then cook over moderate heat until thick enough to coat the back of a spoon, stirring often. Remove the sauce from the heat and stir until cool. Add the brandy and stir well. Use at once or store in the refrigerator. Use within 3 days.

Yield: about 1 quart of sauce

Cranberry-Orange Muffins

I think most American baked goods and desserts are too sweet, but if you like your sugar, raise the amount here to ¾ cup.

2 cups all-purpose flour
3 tablespoons baking powder
1 cup fresh or defrosted cranberries
1 cup milk
2 teaspoons finely grated orange zest
1 large egg
3 tablespoons unsalted butter, softened
1 teaspoon cinnamon
½ cup sugar, or slightly more to taste
½ teaspoon salt

Preheat the oven to 400°F. In a large bowl, whisk together the flour and baking powder. In another large bowl, place the cranberries, milk, orange zest, egg, butter, cinnamon, sugar, and salt. With an immersion blender, pulse the mixture, stirring, until the cranberries are finely chopped.

Spoon the batter into 18 medium muffin paper cups. Bake for 25 minutes.

Yield: 18 medium muffins

INDEX